the mindset
a 31-day metamorphosis

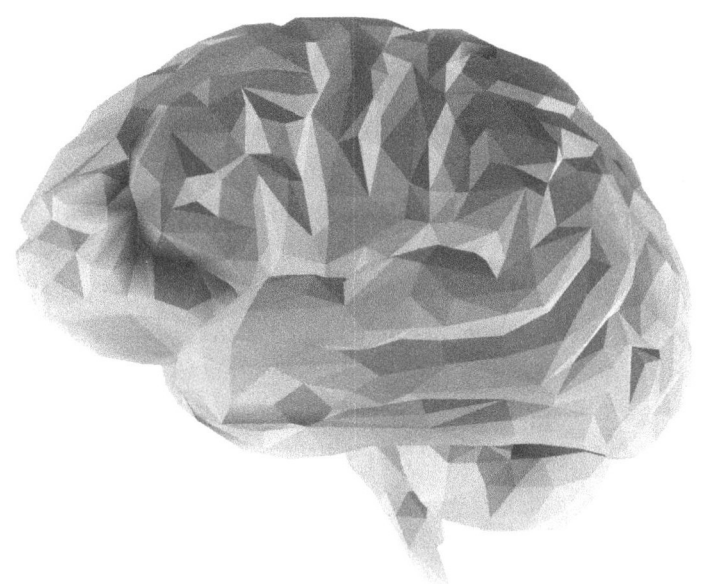

health love money success

Mayura Shekatkar

Copyright © 2020 by Mayura Shekatkar

All rights reserved. No part of this publication may be reproduced, distributed or transmitted in any form or by any means, including photocopying, recording or other electronic or mechanical methods, without the prior written permission of the publisher, except in the case of brief quotations embodied in reviews and certain other non-commercial uses permitted by copyright law.

Printed in the United States of America

Print I!   !90898

E-Book   1490911

Canoe Tree Press

4697 Main Street

Manchester Center, VT 05255

Canoe Tree Press is a division of DartFrog Books.

DEDICATED TO YOU

God has given us small eyes, but they have the power to see the whole sky at once. Similarly, having a limited belief and low self-esteem is an insult to the powerful mindset given to us.

—Mayura

CONTENTS

Acknowledgments 7
My Journey 8
Do You Believe in Your Dreams? 12
Mindpower 14
Believe in Yourself! 18
Day 1: Dreams 20
Day 2: Direction 24
Day 3: Decision 29
Day 4: How Blissful Are You? 34
Day 5: Gratitude is Life 39
Day 6: The Relationship 43
Day 7: Health 47
Day 8: Money 52
Day 9: Your Work 56
Day 10: Way Out of Negativity 60
Day 11: The Element 65
Day 12: Foundation of Abundance Mindset 68
Day 13: Power of Imagination 73
Day 14: Good Morning 77
Day 15: The People 81
Day 16: Miracles Happen Overnight 86
Day 17: Every Day Is a Blessing 91
Day 18: Heal Your Relationships 95
Day 19: Health Is a Gift 101
Day 20: Money Magnet Mindset 106
Day 21: Manifest Your Desire 112
Day 22: Create Your Own Happiness 117

Day 23: Mind and Heart! 122
Day 24: Outcomes 125
Day 25: Your Mind Will Make It Reality................. 130
Day 26: Joy of Giving.. 134
Day 27: Success Is My Destiny................................ 138
Day 28: Mistakes Are Blessings 142
Day 29: All About You 147
Day 30: Mindset Is Everything................................ 151
Day 31: Commanding Your Future......................... 155
How to Break the Worry Habit 159
The Mindset Hero 162
About the Author... 163
Endnotes.. 164

ACKNOWLEDGMENTS

When I started writing this book during the pandemic time of 2020, I had been struggling since 2016 to make ends meet while living in the USA. I made a few wrong choices in my life due to lack of correct direction, but those mistakes made me the strong person I am today. I am very happy to share with the world how I became motivated to see life optimistically when for 25 years back in India I thought that life was terrible. It took me almost six years to fully overcome that bad feeling about life, change my mindset and start experiencing life's blessings. This book is an effort to help people who want to enjoy their life blessings. It's about shaping your mindset in a way that will change your circumstances. There are so many good things I have manifested in my life with the help of gratitude and an optimistic mindset.

This book focuses on the mental ability to manifest things in the material world. When I heard people say, "If you don't like your life, you can change it," I used to think 'Hah! Your life is what it is.' Not anymore. What I discovered is that a buoyant state of mind is a very important aspect of human life. Your thoughts become things. One should be very careful in controlling your thoughts to win over any adverse situation in your life. Your mind has the ability to bring anything to reality. All you need to live a happy, rich, and successful life is the right mindset.

"Leading yourself begins with managing your mindset".

MY JOURNEY

---

*"Life is all about three magical words:
grateful, thankful and blessed!"*
—Mayura Shekatkar

I grew up in a middle-class family in Mumbai, India. I used to hear only complaints, stories of bad experiences from family members. I started believing from an early age that life is too difficult. My mom in particular had a very negative approach to everything even though she was a housewife with a servant to look after the household. She would start her day with a bad mood every morning and just keep talking about how many bad things were happening in the house. Growing up with all that negativity around me impacted my mindset and self-esteem. Is it any wonder I never did well academically? Is it a surprise I didn't see life as something to be enjoyed? My daddy used to say, "Get an education. Get a job." He made me think getting a job would be the end of all my worries, and that isn't true. You must enjoy and love your job. If it's also financially rewarding, that's a bonus. But I just took any job after completing my postgrad studies because of my mindset limit.

Then my surroundings changed a little bit, and I met people who talked about growth and career paths. I started reading books about how to develop a better mindset. I ignored the negatives surrounding me and fed my mind with growth, opportunities and success stories. Little by little, optimism crept into my life. I came across

MY JOURNEY

Soumya who was my supervisor and is a great pal today. She gave me a mug with the quote 'If your dreams don't scare you, they're not big enough!' That day I decided to focus on my dreams very seriously. I was about to discover one of life's little mysteries; the one that says that life is full of opportunities. Miss one and there'll be another along very soon. But you can't take them until you see them. Opportunities? I don't think I knew they existed, but now, with my changed mindset, I did.

And here was the very first I took, "The opportunity to fly abroad to study. I took a chance, resigned from my job in India, and invested everything I'd saved in six years of earning to take a diploma in the USA. It was a hard decision. My father apart, no-one in the family supported it. But I didn't regret it because, when I landed in America, I found the place was full of optimistic people. I developed a habit of gratitude and my life improved.

At the age of twenty-two, I knew I wanted to get out of India, but I lacked direction and decisiveness, and so I was stuck where I was. It took me four years to find a way to go abroad and that got me an American diploma which landed me a job in a startup company that soon closed. I was in debt. You know that saying, 'When the going gets tough, the tough get going'? I wouldn't have called myself tough...I was in for a surprise. Maybe it was knowing the only option was forward. I enrolled in school again for a master's degree. I worked on campus and did a baby-sitting job for a friend to earn money. Being useless at planning, I was just able to make ends meet.

Then, on July 2, 2019, I made the second life-changing decision. No more secondary jobs – I would focus on one well-paid job which I enjoyed. The moment I decided it my mindset started focusing on that well-paid job in the USA. All I thought about was achieving my dream job. I put all my heart and belief into the search for my dream job – and I put something else, too. Something worth more than all the rest. Faith. Faith that my plans would be rewarded. That I'd get the job I dreamed of.

THE MINDSET

Even though I didn't have a job, I followed a working person's schedule. I woke up early every morning. I sat in one place every weekday and applied for jobs from nine in the morning till five in the afternoon, with just 30 minutes in the middle for lunch. Studying and all other chores had to be done outside those hours.

Hard? You bet it was hard. But it paid off. My subconscious mind accepted that I was working 9:00 to 5:00 in a well-paid job in a corporate office. Within 31 days, a well-known company in Boston, Mass offered me a job.

Triumph! Well…no. It should have been, but… after a gap of one and a half years, and disconnected from the practice of mindset gratitude, I let doubt that I could settle once more in the corporate world overcome me.

There is an eternal law called "Something in return." (There is no law called," Something for nothing." Something for nothing does not exist – you can achieve whatever you want to achieve, but you must understand that everything comes in return for something). And so, having got this job in the first 21 days, I lost it in the next 31 days.

But all was not lost – because all is never lost for anyone prepared to learn the lessons Life hands out. In this job, I discovered what I enjoyed about work. I suffered a financial crunch so big that just buying food to live was difficult, but I decided to work hard to get back to the corporate job. I returned to the interview game – and I landed my dream job. During the 2020 pandemic, with companies shutting down and so many people jobless, I was earning well working flexibly from home at the job I enjoy most.

"Never underestimate yourself, you are a gift to this world!"

I was disconnected from my practice of gratitude for a while when I lost that first job. I got back on track with gratitude practice during December 2019. I had always wished to visit Chicago at Christmastime but never had enough money. Well, never mind that! I packed my bag and kept it in my room as if I was about to travel. Whenever I had time, I looked at pictures of Chicago on my computer and my mobile. I edited my picture in front of the Chicago Bean and looked at it many times to feel the happiness that, Yes! I am in Chicago. Around Christmas Eve I told one of my best friends how much I wanted to visit Chicago, and she said, "I have unused air miles to cover your round trip – and they won't be carried forward to next year. I will book your air ticket!"

I was so happy – even though I knew Chicago was still a far-off dream because staying in a hotel or Airbnb would be costly at that time of the year and I didn't have the money. Then, another friend Priyanka who was a Chicago resident invited me to stay with her for the new year. It happened miraculously!

And that's how I was able to put away the edited picture of me in front of the Chicago Bean – I replaced it with the real picture. Just as I had imagined. Hold on to that – it happened just as I had imagined. And what you imagine can happen for you in just the same way.

Correcting my gratitude practice changed my mindset, and changing my mindset changed my life. With years of gratitude practice, I started experiencing the magical moments around me and seeing the many miracles in my life. They're in yours, too – but do you see them? Are your eyes open? Do you look at your life as the blessing it is?

"Never underestimate your power to change yourself."
—H. Jackson Brown

DO YOU BELIEVE IN YOUR DREAMS?

"Don't underestimate yourself. You are capable of more than you can ever imagine."
—Les Brown

Think about the wonderful time of your childhood, where every day feel like magic. Your mindset was full of joy and the enjoyment of life. The only worry was which flavor of ice cream to choose in the ice cream parlor. All you wanted was toys, candy, and food. Life felt exactly like the fairy tales your grandparents told you. You went to bed in a happy mood and woke up with joy thinking only about what you were going to do with this new day. Throwing a rock in the water was exciting. You lived your dream every day.

That's how it is as a small child. And then we grow into adults. Responsibilities, life experiences, difficult situations take their toll. Our belief in "fairy tale life" fades away[1]. We still love to be around kids because for a moment we forget our worries and feel that joy again in our hearts.

It doesn't have to be that way. Dreams can still become reality. It's up to you – and your mindset. The dreams are as real as you are. Life can be more thrilling and awesome than you dare imagine[2]. When you know what to do to bring forth the belief, you will wonder how you ever could have given up in believing in the blessing of life![3]

You may not see fairies flying around you, but you will see things your wishes coming true easily. The things you always dream of are happening easily and effortlessly to bring more joy into your life. You have to believe in your dreams. You can live your dream life. All you have to do is convince your mind and heart it is possible. Life is magical! Life is a blessing! Life is an exciting journey![4]

Are you ready to experience the excitement of life again? Are you ready to be filled every day with the awe and wonder you knew as a kid? Get ready to make your dream of life a reality. Have faith in your abilities and mindset. Believe!

MINDPOWER

"You are what you believe yourself to be."
—Paulo Coelho

Our subconscious mind is working day and night. It reacts to the emotions and stimuli that reach out to it through the different senses of our body. Our subconscious mind is very closely connected to the infinite intelligence which is also known as the law of attraction[5]. What we imagine gets absorbed by our subconscious mind which starts acting to bring it to reality. If you are facing a problem in achieving your dream it will come up with the solutions in the form of situation, people, and experience which will solve the problem.

Whatever it is we want starts with a thought. Mix emotions and feelings and the subconscious mind kicks into action. There are fourteen major emotions, seven positive and seven negative[6]. Positive and negative emotions cannot exist in our minds at the same time[7] – so the solution is obvious. Train your mind to be home to positive emotions. No, having only positive emotions isn't easy. It requires habit and persistence. But once you've got there, you will know infinite success in life. It won't even be true that the sky is the limit, because there will *be* no limit. Let's look at these positive and negative emotions so you will communicate and feed your subconscious mind only with the positive emotions.

The Seven major positive emotions[8]:

1. **DESIRE**
2. **ENTHUSIASM**
3. **FAITH**
4. **HOPE**
5. **LOVE**
6. **ROMANCE**
7. **SEX**

The Seven major negative emotions:

1. **ANGER**
2. **FEAR**
3. **GREED**
4. **HATRED**
5. **JEALOUSY**
6. **REVENGE**
7. **SUPERSTITION**

To have a happy mindset you must get rid of negative emotions. These negative emotions not only harm our mindset power but also affect our body and bring bad life experiences. These negative emotions not only harm one person but our society and, ultimately, our world. Of course, you cannot master a positive mindset just like that! It requires the habit and persistence that you are going to learn in the coming thirty-one days.

Only one emotion at a time dominates your thoughts and mind so it is your responsibility to train your mind to have an optimistic emotion to experience the blessing of life. If we master removal from our mind of all seven negative emotions, we will attain a true state as children of infinite intelligence[9]. Your mind is emitting emotions on a given frequency. It does it all the time, whether you know it or not. The universe receives those emotions and transmits back on the same frequency. Send out despair, despair is what you'll get back. So, send out love. Send out hope. Send out faith. You'll be repaid over and over again.

The shape your life takes follows the way you think. Our mindset is like clay which we need to shape carefully with positive emotions and thoughts to have a positive life experience. So, let's get your mindset clear or all old thoughts and beliefs and get ready to feed it with happy life experiences. William James said, "The greatest discovery of my generation is that it can alter their lives by altering their attitudes of mind. Our thoughts possess dynamic power which helps to shape our mindset. If you want to change your circumstances, correct your thinking first."[10]

A positive mindset creates a positive environment around you to provide you with a pleasant and happy experience.[11] A negative mindset does the opposite. You have to understand that your thoughts are the primary cause of everything that happens in your life[12]. Change your thoughts and mindset and your life experience will change. Don't accept any adverse circumstances. You have to create in your mindset a clear picture of how you want your life to be. Make that picture a very clear note and write every detail about it. Believe in it.

You have to believe and imagine the best possible scenario for any situation. Then expect it and it will happen. All you need to change your life is a mindset, optimistic emotion, and belief – and all of that you already have within you! Isn't it amazing?

The first three days in this book are designed for long term dream achievement. However, just to experience the changed mindset you can start by setting small things like getting a job, a promotion, finding the perfect partner, improving relationships, improving health and fitness, finding the perfect business idea, finance for the business or service you want to start. The first three days will build a foundation for long-term success you want to achieve with your correct mindset.

BELIEVE IN YOURSELF!

"We are what we think. All that we are arises with our thoughts. With our thoughts, we make our world."
—Buddha

To get what we want, we must have control over our mind and our thoughts. We can learn to use our imagination to think about the things we want in our life; once we've mastered it, physical counterparts of those ideas will appear in our life in unexpected ways. When you want something, all the universe conspires in helping you to achieve it. In this process you have to give something in return though your mindset which is known as gratitude power. If we take things for granted then we are not giving back gratitude and the good things stop coming.

You can create the life you want. To do so, you have to gain control of your thoughts. All negative emotions like fear, failure, and doubts are ignited in your mind and your mind rules you. Take control of your mind and thoughts. Every day, bit by bit, watch your thoughts. As soon as a negative thought comes into your mind replace it with a good thought. You must hold a bright, happy, and successful vision of yourself and do not allow fears to interfere with your future successes and achievements. Believe that prosperity is possible in all areas of your life. You are going to learn how to take control of your mindset in this thirty-one-day practice.

Your feelings are always monitoring your thoughts for you. We all know about gut feeling; it is an intuition of your mindset which is telling you what is right and what is wrong. Once you become conscious of how you are feeling, then you become aware of your thoughts. Your mindset is always there to guide you – all you have to do is listen. If your mindset is full of good thoughts and transmitting good feelings to the universe, the universe will return better life experiences to you.

Contrary to what you may read, the universe is not indifferent. It wants what is good for you. We all are born with the mindset power to live in abundance. When we encounter a bad situation, we are blind to the good underneath it. Analyze bad situations carefully and you will see the good things hidden in them. It takes time to train your mindset to see good in every situation. That's what you are going to learn in this book. Trust that every circumstance in your life has a purpose for you. It is there to develop your skills for a better future.

Your mindset has the power to change any negative situation to positive, but you cannot do it by resisting change. Unintentionally many times we focus on the negative, pain, and misery. We are not aware of what is exactly a negative emotion. We can't eliminate negative emotions and feelings from our minds until we have understood them. You have to choose the positive path, and you do that by commanding your mind to see good in everything.

DAY 1
DREAMS

> *"Dreams become reality when we put our minds to it."*
> —Queen Latifah

"I have a dream." Four of the most famous words ever spoken. It's fifty-seven years since Martin Luther King told us he had a dream and the dream would cost him his life – but it changed the world. Twenty years before that speech, there were people facing appalling threats who only survived because they kept their dream alive. That's what dreams can do – that is their power. Throughout history, dreams have kept human beings alive. The world regarded many people as fools as it watched them chasing their dreams – and then their dreams became reality and the ridicule stopped. It doesn't matter who you are, what your current situation, what the circumstances that surround you: Stay faithful to your dreams and every adverse situation will change for the better. It may take time. That's all right. You have time.

A dream is a strong desire one wants to bring to reality. Repeated in your brain enough times, your subconscious mind accepts it as true and makes it reality. Your dream is your responsibility. The world-famous author Napoleon Hill said, "Quitters never win, and Winners never quit."[13] Fix this sentence in your mind. You might get tired on your journey – and that's okay. Rest, get your energy back, and start again. It won't just happen. Achieving your dream needs imagination, but it also needs a plan and then it needs action to bring success into your life. As you work your way through this book, all these things will be made clear.

Thomas Edison lit up the world – but only after he had failed 10,000 times to make a light bulb. He didn't quit. And nor did his mother and that, too, is a story worth remembering. He came home from school one day and handed his mother a letter from school. Her eyes filled with tears as she read the letter out loud to her child: Your son is a genius. This school is too small for him and doesn't have enough good teachers to train him. Please teach him yourself. And so she did; she homeschooled her son and supported all his dreams. Many years after her death, by which time Edison was one of the greatest inventors of his and any other century, he was looking through his mother's old things and found that letter. What it actually said was: "Your son is addled (mentally ill). We cannot let him come to school anymore." Edison cried for hours and then wrote in his diary, "Thomas Alva Edison was an addled child who, thanks to a hero mother, became the genius of the century."

We don't all have that supportive environment, and nor do we have that level of need – but we do (or we should) have a dream that seems impossible to achieve and we do need faith in our ability to achieve anything. Without that mindset, you will find it very difficult to turn your dreams into reality. No matter where you are today and what your situation, your belief and faith in your dreams will set you on the way to achieving everything you want[14].

Write down your dreams and seek the help you need from your teachers, parents, friends, and the internet. Educate yourself to draw up an action plan to achieve your dream. It is not done in one night; it requires persistence and patience. Tim Fargo said, "Who you are tomorrow begins with what you do today." He also said, "Patience and persistence are the providers of progress." You can start at any point in your life. I decided to change my career at the age of 31. I had a degree and professional experience in a field I did not enjoy. I had spent my youth and 10 years of adult life in education and a career forced on me because of social stigma, but when I changed my path, I took full responsibility for my dreams and action.

You are the one who can shape your mindset to turn your dreams into reality[15]. You are your biggest supporter in life[16]. If you have supportive parents, a supportive partner and/or supportive children and grandchildren (I did say at *any* time in your life) then you are lucky but, even if you don't have those things, you still have the capacity to develop your mindset to draw a favorable environment around you. It is a proven fact that a shark in a fish tank will only grow to eight inches long but, in the ocean, it will grow to more than eight feet[17]. Similarly, no-one grows when surrounded by small-thinking people. You are not a shark; you are a human being and you have a better brain and greater thinking power. Surround yourself with people with optimism and a growth mindset. If you find yourself in an environment unfavorable to change, then start by changing your mindset and change in the things around you will follow.

"It doesn't matter how big your dream is. All you need is YOU!"

DAY 1 TASKS

1. Make a list of the dreams you want to achieve.
2. You can list dreams for the coming week, the next year or the coming decade.
3. List the resources and the education you need to make your dreams reality. This may take time, because you probably need to research it, but don't stop. Stopping is how dreams remain dreams and fail to become reality.
4. Don't tell anyone about your dreams until they have become reality.
5. Till you finish the practice in this book, say no negative words and have no negative thoughts about yourself or anyone else.
6. Only read one chapter each day and complete the task on that day itself. Do not read the next chapter unless the day's task list tells you to.

Note: in case you miss a day then go back three days and continue from there. Remember: any negativity around you or negative thought in your mind is affecting your ability to be a successful person.

DAY 2
DIRECTION

"There are dreamers and there are planners; the planners make their dreams come true."
—Edwin Louis Cole

Yesterday you made a list of your dreams. Those dreams are now your goals and you are ready to plan a road map to follow your dreams. Always remember: When you encounter failure, change your plan and not your goal. This practice will help you along your journey to be a successful person. If you are looking to be specialized in a job or business, acquire the necessary knowledge by educating yourself with the help of others[18]. You must have like-minded people around you. Think of this as building your mastermind groups. The best example of a mastermind group is a law firm in which lawyers who specialize in different fields work together. When a new case comes in, they discuss it together to find the best solution to the problem. In my life, I had no plan till I reached the age of 26. I decided to move to the USA to study and, when I got here, I struggled to combine study, a part-time job and chores. What's more, I had to maintain good health because I could not afford medical cover . My academic advisor and teacher helped me plan my day so effectively, I even managed to squeeze some spare time out of a schedule that included school, part-time job, gym, and house chores and I spent that free time interacting with students from different cultural backgrounds with growth and success mindset. "Master Minds," in fact. And they helped me to be firm in action.

Organized planning is vital[19]. It helps you see the barriers in your way while you still have time to find a solution. To do that you need to add a group of mastermind people to provide you with expert guidance when you need it[20]. If you are planning a business, you will also need investors. If you are planning to land your dream job, you need to find the company you want to work for. If you have to move to a different location, then plan how you are going to make it happen.

Planning is one step towards your dream. But you also need a Plan B – and maybe Plans C, D and E, too – in case things don't go smoothly[21]. Try to make a flawless plan in one attempt itself. Once your plan is ready then you are blind to failure. Let's consider a list of different dreams:

1. **Start a business**
    1.1   What kind of business do you want to start?
    1.2   What does success in that business look like?
    1.3   If it is not suitable for the current location or customers, then identify the target customer base?
    1.4   Do you have enough funding to start the business?
    1.5   If you don't have enough money, then can you work with someone in partnership or get a loan to start your business?
    1.6   Do you need a physical space for your business, or will you make it online?
    1.7   Marketing strategies for your business / product?
    1.8   Competition in your business or do you have a new and unique idea?
    1.9   How many employees do you need for your business?
    1.10 What is the initial profit margin?

THE MINDSET

2 **Start a service**

    2.11   What kind of service do you want to offer your customers?

    2.12   Is anyone else providing a similar service?

    2.13   How you will make your service unique?

    2.14   How will you deliver this service?

    2.15   How can you collect customer feedback to make your service better?

    2.16   What is the initial amount you need to start this service?

    2.17   How are you going to market your service?

    2.18   What industry is the service in and what scope is there for growth?

    2.19   What is your initial target for Quarter 1?

    2.20   What is the profit margin?

3 **Dream job**

    3.21   What type of job do you want to do?

    3.22   Do you have the necessary skill set?

    3.23   Do you have a required qualification?

    3.24   What career growth opportunities are there if you choose this job?

    3.25   Is it a seasonal job?

    3.26   Which company do you want to work for?

    3.27   What is the market salary of this type of job?

    3.28   If you don't have enough skills and education, then who can be your mentor to achieve the dream job?

    3.29   How you are going to prepare your resume?

3.30 On which professional sites do you want to market your resume?

Figure out answers to the above question and head in the right direction. Remember these are sample questions, your question list can be bigger than this depending upon your dream. You have to find out related material in the area in which you want to be successful. I know not all jobs and industries make good money but if you are unique and come up with creative ideas you'll be fine. Do you have to fix up your mindset about what you want to achieve? How much money do you want to make? Where do you want to see yourself in the next 5 years?

There are so many industries that are not explored completely and do have scope to be the first market players. Jeff Bezos started Amazon.com as a simple online book library service in Bellevue, WA with very little money and a few books from the collection on his shelf. Today, Amazon is the world's number one e-commerce company. When he came up with an idea it was new and unique, but his mindset was focused on growing his service which made him the most successful person in business today. Similarly, there are many ideas your mind can produce which will make you a successful person – but only if, when you have decided where you want to be, you work out a way to get there.

When I decided to go abroad, I had no financial support. All I had was the dream of going abroad. I started looking for opportunities within the company and other study opportunities. With a full-time job, I have managed to spend 3-4 hours every day studying to fulfill my dream. My mind was focused on fulfilling my dream, and the right people and opportunities presented themselves. Four months later, I landed in the USA. That's what happens when you focus.

ALL THAT MATTER IS YOUR MINDSET FOR THE SUCCESS!

DAY 2 TASKS

1. List the job, business or service you want to achieve.
2. Write a definite plan to achieve your dream.
3. Don't focus on how things will unfold; fix in your mind a clear picture of your achievement as often as you can.
4. Don't tell anyone about your dream until it becomes reality.
5. Till you finish the practice in this book, don't say any negative words or think a negative thought about yourself or anyone else.
6. Read only one chapter each day and complete the task on that day itself.

DAY 3
DECISION

*"Sometimes it's the smallest decisions
that can change your life forever."*
—Keri Russell

Pat yourself on the back because you are making progress in achieving your dreams though action, plan and decision. That decision is the third and most important step. Our mind has the ability to do noble or terrible things[22]. Life is only as good as your mindset. The side of the equation we end up on depends on our decision, not on the conditions or people around us. Our mind consists of two ways of decision making. The first is known as "Higher-self" and leads us to success[23]. The second is known as "Lower-self" and generates an adequate mindset. But who wants to settle for adequate? You are going to develop your mindpower to guide your subconscious mind to become the best version of yourself because your higher self is blind to failure – it just can't see or imagine it[24]. Instead, it focuses on standard situations and draws out favorable results. The lower-self, on the other hand, is into procrastination and fear of failure. We need to forget about fear. Fear is nothing but lack of power to control our minds, a fuel that influences our decisions and sends us down incorrect alleyways to avoid unwanted situations.

Don't be influenced by the opinions of others. You have your own brain and your own mind; use them to make your own decisions[25]. If you aren't sure about the decision, seek help from people who understand the subject. The biggest thing a successful person can have is silence on his lips and a smile on his face[26]. The first principle to develop a successful mindset is a decision to keep your mouth shut, listen, and observe more[27]. Do not share your future plans about business and services with everyone. Try it before you show it to the world. Your focus should be forward. There is abundance for each one of us. Fast and accurate decisions will make us successful. It takes time to develop decision skills. You must have the courage to fully commit to your dream.

Colonel Harland Sanders, the founder of KFC, made a decision to sell the best chicken in Kentucky. He made that decision after his retirement, which many might think too late – but he persisted and, when he was 62, KFC become famous – in Kentucky. He decided to extend that fame world-wide; when he was 75, he sold his company for billions of dollars. You can make your decisions at any point in your life. Each decision made breeds more self-confidence. **Trust that things are always working out for your good. When your decision has the desired outcome, you generate trust in your abilities; that's WINNING. When your choices have unwanted results, you learn who you are; that's WISDOM. Both helps you grow and master how to get life right. Every decision cultivates your discernment and helps you level up**[28]. Even when you've mastered deciding, you still need persistence to carry it forward and achieve success.

Is making a good decision enough to achieve success and happiness in life? Not without persistence[29]. Persistence restores faith in your abilities to overcome challenging situations. <u>Persistence is nothing but a state of mind based on the following factors:</u>

1. **SPECIFIC PURPOSE**: knowing exactly what you want and making it clear in your mind is a very important step to develop persistence. A strong desire forces you to overcome any difficulty[30].

2. **FAITH IN DREAMS**: faith in your dreams helps you to develop the persistence to move forward in life.
3. **BELIEF**: belief in your ability will encourage you to follow the plan with persistence.
4. **PRECISE PLANS**: a well-defined plan is very important. Don't hesitate to alter your plan if you find a flaw in it. Correcting your plan is persistence.
5. **EXACT KNOWLEDGE**: logical facts and knowledge help you to encourage persistence. Guessing is harmful to your mindset and destroys persistence.
6. **TEAMWORK**: One must have a harmonious relationship with others. You can learn from anyone. Understanding and sympathy towards others help to develop persistence.
7. **DETERMINATION**: A strong will to develop your plans to achieve the desired success leads to persistence.
8. **HABIT**: Our mindset depends on the daily experience upon which it feeds. Regular practice makes it your habit and eventually helps you to master persistence.

With all the above factors, you are shaping your mindset to take quick and accurate decisions to bring more success and happiness in your life and the surrounding people.

Let's see quickly how to develop persistence. Below is a list of four simple steps that lead to the habit of persistence[31]:

1. A STRONG DREAM BACKED BY THE PLAN OF ACTION FOR ITS FULFILLMENT.
2. A WELL-DESIGNED PLAN BACKED BY ACTION.
3. A MINDSET BLIND TO NEGATIVITY, FEAR, AND THE NEGATIVE OPINIONS OF OTHERS.

4. COLLABORATION WITH THE PEOPLE WHO WILL INFLUENCE YOUR ACTION TO FOLLOW THE PLAN AND ACHIEVE YOUR DREAM.

"Making good decisions is a crucial skill at every level."
—Peter Drucker

DAY 3 TASKS

1. Make a decision to commit to your dream.
2. Read your dreams and action plan early in the morning and before going to bed at night.
3. List what you did today to achieve your dreams.
4. List names of the people who can help you develop a plan of action and find funding and resources you need for your business, job or service.
5. Do not tell anyone about your dreams until they become reality.
6. Till you finish the practice in this book, don't say any negative words or think a negative thought about yourself or anyone else.

DAY 4
HOW BLISSFUL ARE YOU?

"Reflect upon your present blessings-of which every man has many-not on your past misfortunes, of which all men have some."
—Charles Dickens

One of the key things you need to remember – perhaps *the* key thing – is this: The Universe is on your side. The Universe *wants* you to be happy. But in return the Universe asks one thing: That you be grateful and make your gratitude clear. Failing to say "Thank You" is the single most common cause for losing Life's blessings. And so, to share fully in Life's bounty, you have to master the art of showing – and *feeling* – gratitude. Day 4 is when you learn to do that.

Our thoughts become things and hence we are focusing on developing a mindset with a blissful heart. The thankful heart opens our eyes to a multitude of blessings that continually surround us. This is the basic principle for you to master today. Counting how blissful you are in different areas of your life will help you to shape a better opportunity or bring more success into your life. Among all the feelings that can change your life, being grateful for what you already have is the biggest. When you are thankful for whatever you have no matter how small it is, it will multiply. If, you are grateful for one dollar in your pocket you will attract more money. When you are grateful for the family or spouse, even if the love is not overwhelming, you will see that relationship as a blessing. If you have a job which is not your dream job, be grateful for it and soon that feeling will lead you to your dream job.

When you are not grateful for the things you already have then you are trapped into negative feelings towards everything around you and those negative feelings will attract more negative experiences into your life. Soon your mindset will believe that life is miserable and not a blessing. Every negative feeling in your mind generates a bad feeling in your heart and takes you away from the blessing. Every time you have a negative thought then remind yourself: Am I willing to lose my blessings for this bad feeling? Finding fault in other people or things is a form of negativity. Jealousy is a negative emotion. If others can achieve something, so can you. Saying "I don't have enough" or "I am always running late" is a negative feeling moving you away from a blissful life. **I have tried both counting my blessings and counting negative things, and I assure you that counting your blessing is the only way to bring success into your life**[32]. **So, promise yourself today: "I choose to believe in sudden miracles and unexpected blessings."**

First thing in the morning as soon as you open your eyes say thank you three times that you woke up to see this beautiful world again. Make a journal or type on your computer or laptop every morning ten things you are grateful for. Don't just list the thing itself but write your reason for being grateful because thinking about the reason develops a strong feeling in your mind. How strongly you feel will determine how strongly you work to change your mindset and your life entirely.

Here are some examples of blessing counting[33]:

I am blessed to have _____, because_____.

I grateful to have_____, because_____.

From the bottom of my heart I am thankful for_____ because_____.

I am very happy & blessed to have_____, because___.

THE MINDSET

Once you finish writing your blessings then go back and read them aloud and after each blessing say "Thank you! Thank you! Thank you!". Feel grateful from the bottom of your heart. To generate the feeling of more gratitude you can thank God, the Universe, Divine guidance, your higher self, Life, or anything you like – just so long as it helps make your feeling of gratitude strong.

Counting your blessings is very simple yet very powerful[34]. It stimulates in the subconscious mind the realization that you have an abundance. Feeling grateful makes your mind more active. Till you finish the practice in this book you have to count 10 new blessings every morning. It is hard to find new things every day, but you have to think about what makes you more blissful. The more gratitude you have, the more your mindset is calm and clears. You can be grateful for your family, friends, job, pets, the beauty of nature, services you receive or received in the past, the air you breathe, the water you drink, the food you eat, your body and its great immune system, all your organs because without all of them you won't be alive. If you can't add ten new things every day then just be grateful for the things you remember.

Soon you will find you feel happier and more joyful every time you count your blessings. It stimulates your mindset to be grateful for the things you have. The more gratitude you express, the more things will come to you. Your mind will become a magnet to bring more blessings into your life. Some days you will feel happy very quickly; on others it may take longer[35]. You should continue counting your blessing every day and you will see your life will change drastically better than you ever imagined.

Mindset powerful subject to be grateful for:

1) Health

2) Job

3) Relationship

4) Money

5) Career

6) Passion

7) Happiness

8) Kids

9) Love

10) Life

11) Pets

12) Nature: earth, air, water and sun

13) Material goods and services

Our mindset shapes our life based on three magical words "GRATEFUL, THANKFUL AND BLESSED!"

DAY 4 TASKS

1. First thing in the morning, make a list of ten blessing in your life to be grateful for.
2. Write the reason why you are grateful for each blessing.
3. Read your list aloud and say "Thank you" three times after you read each blessing. Close your eyes and feel gratitude from the bottom of your heart as much as you can.
4. Repeat the above three steps of this practice till you complete thirty-one days in this book.
5. For the next 31 days, don't say any negative words or think a negative thought about yourself or anyone else.
6. ****Read tomorrows practice today because you need to do something specific before you start your day tomorrow.**

DAY 5
GRATITUDE IS LIFE

"Gratitude makes sense of our past, brings peace for today, and creates a vision for tomorrow."
—Melody Beattie

Gratitude is a good feeling and accumulating a series of good feelings every day will help you to develop a mindset. You have to follow tasks 4 and 5 every day until you complete this book. We are making a habit of going back to sleep and waking up in a happy mood[36]. Gratitude does a lot for our brains and mental well-being. Practicing gratitude before going to bed will help you to sleep better and longer. It will enhance your self-esteem, which is an important factor in your mindset, attitude, and personality. Practicing gratitude for a long time will increase your mental strength. Research shows that people who practice gratitude every day get a number of benefits[37]:

1) IMPROVED PHYSICAL HEALTH

2) IMPROVED SLEEP

3) IMPROVED PSYCHOLOGICAL HEALTH

4) INCREASED EMPATHY

5) REDUCED AGGRESSION

6) MORE SOCIAL CONNECTION

7) ENHANCED SELF-ESTEEM

8) IMPROVED MENTAL STRENGTH

THE MINDSET

There are different things you can try to express gratitude:

1) **GRATITUDE ROCK**: go to a garden, river, or any place where you can find a small rock that fits into your palm and you can hold easily in your closed fist. It should be smooth and good to feel. You can also use as a gratitude rock any precious stone or crystal you already have. I have a gratitude rock and it is very easy to carry with me if I am traveling. **(This is recommended for your practice because it is very easy to find and carry with you.)**

2) **GRATITUDE JOURNAL**: writing down every day memories for which you are grateful is the easiest way to remember the good things that happened that day. You can keep it on your computer, note pad or phone. If it isn't possible to open your computer every night before going to bed then just note it in an email draft on the phone and paste it in your gratitude journal in the morning. You can also maintain a small physical diary as a gratitude journal.

3) **GRATITUDE BOX**: If you are home or in one place while doing practice in this book then you can take a box or jar and keep it next to your bed which you can see every night before going to bed and early morning when you wake up from the sleep.

4) **GRATITUDE POST RATES**: you can write three things you are grateful every day before going back to bed and stick it next to your bed or you can stick it in a journal and keep it next to your bed.

This practice is very simple: Hold your gratitude rock in your hand tonight before going to bed. Close your eyes and go very carefully through all the good things that happened during the day. Choose 3-4 things you are most grateful for and say thank you three times. If you are using a box or jar at the end of the 31st day read each note and you will realize how many things you already have. The more you think about things to be grateful for, the more you will generate happy feelings in your heart. Good things will start happening faster than you could wish for, and you will start to experience a dynamic change in your life.

The count your blessing and gratitude rock practice will help you to start and end your day with a grateful mindset[38]. Together these practices are very powerful happiness generators. Gratitude is a magnetic force that will bring your wishes, dreams, and things you need to you as if by magic. These two practices over the period of a few months changed my life so completely that I came to see that failure was impossible. The day I learned this practice, it became part of my regular routine and now I have practiced it for four years. This book is designed to give you the same experience in a shorter period. You should continue this practice as long as your dreams and wishes come true and make it a habit for the lifetime.

DAY 5 TASKS

1. Repeat steps one to three of Day 4's task. Count your blessings: Make a list of ten blessings. Write why you're grateful. Reread your list, and at the end of each blessing say thank you, thank you, thank you, and feel as grateful for that blessing as you can.
2. Find a gratitude rock / gratitude journal / gratitude box or jar and put it by your bed where you can see it daily.
3. Before going to bed, hold your gratitude rock in your hand and think of the best things that happened today.
4. Say the words thank you, thank you, thank you from the bottom of your heart for all the good things that happened today.
5. Repeat the gratitude rock practice every night till you complete 31 days.
6. **<u>**READ TOMORROW'S PRACTICE TODAY AS YOU NEED TO COLLECT SOME PHOTOGRAPHS BEFORE YOU BEGIN.</u>**

DAY 6
THE RELATIONSHIP

"We can only be said to be alive in those moments when our hearts are conscious of our treasures."
—Thornton Wilder

The people in our lives give us joy and experience. They give meaning to our life. Or, of course, they don't. Be careful about the company you keep. To develop the right mindset, it is very important to surround yourself with people who help you achieve your dreams, help you find solutions to the obstacles in your life. People with a gratitude mindset have a better relationship with their colleagues, friends, and family[39]. They feel more harmonious in any relationship and that attracts more people to them. Research shows that, for every one complaint about another person, whether in thought or word, it takes ten blessings for the relationship to flourish. Abhorrence is a bad emotional feeling that affects our mindset and the people around us. Married couples who start complaining about each other more end in divorce.

Gratitude helps you to restore harmony in the relationship and ultimately the relationship will flourish. Gratitude towards any relationship develops significant notable changes in your mindset. Gratitude will help you to be more patient, understanding, compassionate, and a kinder person. Every complaint you have about another person will disappear as your mindset is focused only on the good qualities in another person[40].

THE MINDSET

Thinking something is not the same as speaking it out loud. The power of the spoken word is great energy. Your thoughts come out of in the form of words and that builds or destroys the relationship you have. Whatever you say or think about another person, a complaint will come back on you tenfold – and that is why you should not to have or utter a bad thought or word about yourself or anyone else until you have completed the practice in this book. Every negative feeling, bad thought and word affects your life before it impacts the other person. One small matchstick burns itself first before bringing down anything; similarly, one bad feeling, complaint and thought destroys the harmony of life around you.

Today's practice is about being grateful for the relationships you have in your life and the surrounding people just the way they are. Even if all your relationships are harmonious, still be grateful that you have them. It is a blessing to have family, spouse, kids – many people are praying and waiting for it to appear in their lives.

Choose three of your closet relationships to be grateful for. You might choose any particular family member, friend, boyfriend, girlfriend, business partner, colleague. You can choose three relationships which are very important to you. Take a photograph of the other person or of both of you together. It is fine if the person is no more (your grandparents?) – you can still use their photographs. Once you have selected three relationships, take the photograph of each person in your hand or set it in front of you, one at a time, and think about the things you most like about that person. Their kind behavior, motivating words during your hard times, sense of humor, their looks, their dress sense, the food they cook, the outing, the project, or just the quality time you two enjoyed the most. Memories of the support from that person when you were sick, and the care and love they showed you.

List the five things you like best about them. Take your gratitude journal or your computer and list those things carefully. Begin your sentence with the words *thank you*, address the person by their name, and then write what you're grateful for[41].

Thank you, _____, for_____.

For example, "Thank you, Luiza, for always motivating me." OR, "Thank you, Grandma, for all your love."

Once are you have listed five things about each of the three people, take their photos with you and put them in a place where you can see them frequently. If you are traveling, carry their photos in a wallet or on your phone and make an effort to look at them as often as possible. Whenever you look at their photos say, Thank you, and speak the person's name:

Thank you, Luiza.

The more you practice this for any relationship of your choice, the better you will feel. It will generate good emotions about that person and that relationship. It will set seeing good things in a relationship rather than flaws. The more optimistic and grateful you become about it, the more the relationship will flourish. You can use this practice in the same relationship as many times as you want until it becomes good for both of you. You can try using this practice in a different relationship. You have to see the good things in others as much as possible and be thankful for that relationship. The more grateful you are for the relationship in your life, the faster your mindset will change to make your life a blessing.

Remember life revolves around three magical words: "**GRATEFUL, THANKFUL, BLESSED!**"

DAY 6 TASKS

1. Repeat steps one to three of Day 4's task. Count your blessings: Make a list of ten blessings. Write why you're grateful. Reread your list, and at the end of each blessing say thank you, thank you, thank you, and feel as grateful for that blessing as you can.

2. Choose the most important relationships in your life and collect photographs of each person.

3. With the photograph in front of you write the five things you are grateful about that relationship in your journal or on your computer.

4. Write a sentence about each person beginning with Thank you, then the person's name and what specifically you're grateful for.

5. Carry their photograph with you from today onwards or keep it in a place where you can see it frequently. Try to look at these photos and say thank you and that person's name as many as times in a day as possible.

6. Before going to bed, hold your gratitude rock in your hand and say the words thank you, thank you, thank you from the bottom of your heart for all the good things that happened today.

DAY 7
HEALTH

"The first wealth is health."
—Ralph Waldo Emerson

While we have it, most of us take our health for granted. We do pay attention to it when we're sick, but really we should appreciate and be grateful more when we are well. What is the point of wealth without health? How do you expect to enjoy it?

Our mindset and thinking are closely related to how we feel physically. A healthy body needs a happy mind. Our health is our greatest gift. And, if we didn't know that before the 2020 Covid-19 pandemic started – we do now!

Giving thanks for your health is vital. When you start being grateful for the health you have you will develop a mindset that, the law of attraction, will draw abundant health to you. Increasing your mindset power will help you to overcome small aches and pains and other little troubles[42]. You will feel an increase in your energy and stamina, and your happiness will increase.

In later practices you will learn how to focus on your particular health organ to improve it further. The healthier your body is, the happier you feel. The more you express your gratitude for health, the more health will come to you in return.

Gratitude will help you to eliminate the stress and tension in your body. Stress and tension are the root cause of all health issues.

THE MINDSET

Studies show that our mind has tremendous power over the body and how quickly it ages[43]. Many doctors agree that the secret to keeping the body young and healthy is a grateful heart and an optimistic mindset[44]. A positive mindset with gratitude helps lower your anxiety and stress levels and stabilize behavior. Many great people in history have been aware of the power of gratitude to keep their mindset active[45]. They lived full lives that were difficult at times, but they knew how to approach challenges with a positive attitude and not be overwhelmed by the obstacles they faced.

If you feel heavy and life feels like a real effort to get though, or if you don't feel younger than your age, then you are living with decreased health. All this because you are not feeling grateful for your health. Fix your mindset and you will see a change in your body.

Today's practice is about feeling gratitude for your health. You want to focus on a particular part of the body and be grateful for it. Close your eyes and think about each part of your body and feel why you are grateful for it. How it makes your life better. The deeper your gratitude, the better you will feel about it and it will generate good stimuli in your mind. We are going to focus on body parts, but you can also practice it in your organs[46]. You can also give sincere thanks for past recoveries and feel grateful for them.

1. **Brain**: Think about your brain which is functioning 24x7 to produce results in different senses. It comes up with solutions to different problems, stores knowledge and makes it available whenever you need it. It generates innovative ideas in your mind to bring you success. Say, "Thank you for my brain and my beautiful mind!"

2. **Eyes:** Your eyes help you to recognize your loved one's faces and see the beauty of this world. They make your life more comfortable. Blindfold your eyes and try to do your usual routine. Say, "Thank you for my eyes that enable me to see good in everything!"

3. **Ears:** They are very important too because they help you to listen to different voices of the people to communicate effectively. You are able to listen to music, talk on the phone. Since the vehicle coming from a different direction. Say, "Thank you for my good hearing ability."

4. **Senses**

    4.1 **Sense of taste**: with the sense of taste you can taste amazing food, eat and drink. Enjoy the joy of eating fresh fruits. Your joy in food is nothing without a sense of taste. Say, "Thank you for my amazing sense of taste!"

    4.2 **Sense of Smell**: because of your sense of smell you are able to enjoy different fragrances like perfumes, flowers, the smell of soil after rain, and the smell of fire to save yourself from harm. Say, "Thank you for my amazing sense of smell!"

    4.3 **Sense of Touch**: you could not feel an object or express your love or feeling without a sense of touch. Hugging, holding hands, the kiss is the most amazing feeling in the world. Say, "Thank you for my precious sense of touch!"

5. **Hand and arms:** Without your hands, you would depend on others for virtually everything. Say, "Thank you for my arms, hands, and fingers!"

6. **Legs:** In a word: Freedom. Say, "Thank you for my legs and feet to give me joy in my life."

Without your body you have no identity. Your soul lives in your body to give you the joy of life. Say thank you for my healthy and strong heart! Now take a piece of paper or cardboard and write on it in big bold letters:

"MY HEALTH IS MY GREATEST WEALTH"[47]

THE MINDSET

Keep this card with you and read it as often as possible. Keep it in where you will see it often. Every time you see it, read it aloud and say thank you for your health.

Being grateful for your health when you are feeling completely fit is vital to develop a healthy mindset to keep your body healthy. The more you are grateful for your health, the more enjoyable your life will become! Healthy mindset, healthy body gives you joy in the life.

DAY 7 TASKS

1. Repeat steps one to three of Day 4's task. Count your blessings: Make a list of ten blessings. Write why you're grateful. Reread your list, and at the end of each blessing say thank you, thank you, thank you, and feel as grateful for that blessing as you can.

2. On a piece of paper or cardboard write the words in bold letters:

   "MY HEALTH IS MY GREATEST WEALTH."

3. Place this piece of paper where you will see it often and try to read it aloud at least four times today and repeat it every day till you complete the 31st day.

4. Before going to bed, hold your gratitude rock in your hand and say the words thank you, thank you, thank you from the bottom of your heart for all the good things that happened today.

DAY 8
MONEY

"Acknowledging the good that you already have in your life is the foundation for all abundance."
—Eckhart Tolle

Abundance is the natural state. To have plenty is what the universe wants for you. But we can get in the way of our own destiny. Feeling anxious, covetous or useless will affect your mindset and stand in the way of becoming rich[48]. Complaining about the cost, saying I can't afford this and that is too expensive will make your mindset towards money bad. As discussed in earlier chapters, jealousy and fear are negative emotions that affect your mindset. There is a science of getting rich. You must have a rich mindset to bring riches to you[49].

Whatever your current situation is not final. Change your mindset and your situation will change, too. To build future wealth, you must be grateful for the money you have currently or have had in the past[50].

Feeling grateful for money when your financial situation is challenging is very difficult. You have to understand that the more gratefully we fix our minds about good feelings about money the more money will come to us in the near future. The reason simply is that the mental attitude of gratitude draws the mind into closer touch with the source from which the blessing (money) comes[51].

Think about life since the day you were born. Think about the money that's passed through your hands since then – not all of it in cash form, Money, yes, but also food, clothes, toys, books, medical service, all free. Someone paid money for you or you received some money as a gift at Christmas or on a birthday. Think about it and say thank you for the bottom of your heart.

Did you have food to eat?

Did you have clean clothes to wear even though your size was changing quickly?

Did you live at home?

Did you get books and education as a child?

Did you have toys, a bike, or a pet?

Did you go on vacation?

Did you receive medical care when you were sick?

Did you have essentials like soap, toothpaste, toothbrush, shampoo?

Did you have a television, a phone, a car, a bike? Light, electricity, gas?

All these things cost money, and you got them free. As, you travel back through childhood memories you will see the sheer scale of financial benefit in even the poorest homes. The more sincerely you develop a mindset for the money given to you in the past, the more will come to you in the near future. A grateful mind is always focused on the best, and this best feeling in our mind becomes the faith and this faithful gratitude feeling goes out into the universe to bring best to us[52].

To continue to develop a good feeling and mindset about money take the smallest bill you have, and write on a sticker that you place on the bill:

I AM GRATEFUL FOR ALL THE WEALTH I'VE BEEN GIVEN THROUGHOUT MY LIFE[53].

THE MINDSET

That bill just became your abundance bill. Don't spend it. From today onwards, carry it with you, look at it as many times as possible throughout the day, and read the sentence written on it. The more grateful you feel about it the more your mindset will start focusing on good feelings about the money. Soon you will see the changes in your life where money-making opportunities start coming to you. Don't think about how the money will come – just focus on the feeling you already have and feel the joy of having money with a grateful heart.

If you find yourself in a situation where you are complaining about money, remember that each complaint develops negative feelings and takes you away from the abundant flow of money. Gratitude is riches and complaints are poverty[54].

Promise yourself you will not have feelings of envy when you see others with more money than you. Instead, focus on your own riches and be grateful for them. Give sincere thanks for the discounts and the gifts you receive, your salary and anything else that comes your way. Being grateful sets your abundance mindset into motion.

DAY 8 TASKS

1. Repeat steps one to three of Day 4's task. Count your blessings: Make a list of ten blessings. Write why you're grateful. Reread your list, and at the end of each blessing say thank you, thank you, thank you, and feel as grateful for that blessing as you can.

2. Sit down and think about your childhood and all the things that were given to you free of cost which cost money.

3. As you note down each incident where money is paid for you say thank you and feel grateful and good about it.

4. Take a dollar bill or any other bill and put a sticker on with sentence in bold letters: THANK YOU FOR ALL THE WEALTH I'VE BEEN GIVEN THROUGHOUT MY LIFE. This is your abundance bill.

5. Carry your abundance bill with you and look at it as often as possible, read out the sentence on it and feel gratitude for the abundance money given to you.

6. Before going to bed, hold your gratitude rock in your hand and say the words thank you, thank you, thank you from the bottom of your heart for all the good things that happened today.

DAY 9
YOUR WORK

---

*"We are told that talent creates opportunity,
yet it is desire that creates talent."*
—Bruce Lee

Do you wonder how a poor person with no education become a world famous? Do you ever think what made this poor people to be so successful even though they never had a penny in their pocket when they started career? Do you know why? Is their mindset! A neighbor's child is in trouble from childhood and ends on Skid Row at thirty, penniless and friendless. Have you ever seen a two people with same level of education and financial background start career, and one become rich and other end into obscurity?[55] Why? What makes these lives that start so alike end so differently? Chance? The random wheel of Fate? No. It's a question of mindset. Their mindset about what they do and how they focus on their desire for success. Those with a gratitude mindset will know success in life and those who fail to express gratitude for what they have will fail. You must have understood by now that without gratitude it is impossible to bring permanent success into your life. To increase anything in your life, you have to be grateful for what you already have.

To bring success or increase the good things in your job or workplace like promotion, money-making opportunities, creative ideas, growing a business or selling a product or service it is essential to be grateful for what you currently have. If you want to understand the value of your job, try to imagine yourself without it.

When you feel grateful for your job, you automatically give more to your work, and when you give more to your work you naturally attract an increase in the money and success that is returned to you[56]. If you are not grateful for your job, you will automatically give less, and when you give less you reduce what comes back to you. You cannot do well when you don't have a good feeling about your job. The more grateful your mindset is towards the things you have, the more you will have to be thankful for.

1. **Gratitude mindset for Job:** It doesn't matter what job you are doing. Even if it is not your dream job, it's helping to pay your bills and provide food for you and your family so be grateful and do things happily and with a joyful mindset and soon you will see the opportunity that will thrill you with success. As explained on Day 2. keep looking for resources to get into your dream job.

2. **Gratitude mindset for Business:** If you are a business owner then be grateful for your employees, customers and vendors because they are the ones who are supporting your business[57]. The more gratitude you express towards all things related to the business the quicker you will see the business increase.

Imagine a supervisor is making note of how many times you feel grateful for whatever you are doing. The more you develop a gratitude mindset, the faster you will see your situation improve. Never complain about any situation – look instead for an opportunity to learn from it.

Be grateful for your work, even if it isn't your dream job, because lots of people would love to have it. Be grateful for whatever it brings you – your pay-check of course but also any other services you have like AC, heating, phone, free coffee, subsidized or free food at office events, the janitors who keep your desk and office place clean. Never mind the things you don't like – leave complaining about those to others check. Concentrate on good things about your job and note it down.

When your imaginary supervisor notices your gratitude mindset towards work, it will help to lift you above where you are right now.

If this practice falls on the weekend, and if weekends are not a working time for you, then move on to the next day but come back to this practice on Monday and do it sincerely. The better things you notice about your current job your mindset will be developed for the next leveling up and with fewer efforts you will bring success into your work, business. Whatever you do, do it with passion, all your heart and mind so that you become the expert of it.

Before you start today's task, there's something you need to understand. It would be very easy to approach this business of being grateful almost as a form of bribery: "If I keep saying Thank You, the Universe will reward me with lots of money. I'll be rich. Woo hoo!" That is not how it works. Yes, if you show the Universe your gratitude you will be rewarded – but don't carry out these exercises in that spirit. Keep saying Thank You because you want to align yourself with a beneficent Universe. The rewards will come. And you need to know that those rewards may not be in the form you ask for.

A man whose business was struggling adopted the gratitude approach and put a lot of effort into imagining a big lottery win. That was how he saw his problems ending. Well, he never did win the lottery – but his problems did end. New earnings opportunities he'd never seen before kept presenting themselves. He ended up rich – but the Universe made him work for it. A prayer said in the right way will always be answered, but the answer will rarely be in the form the person praying expects[58].

DAY 9 TASKS

1. Repeat steps one to three of Day 4's task. Count your blessings: Make a list of ten blessings. Write why you're grateful. Reread your list, and at the end of each blessing say thank you, thank you, thank you, and feel as grateful for that blessing as you can.

2. Note down at least ten good things about your current job or business and say thank you for it with all of your heart.

3. While at work remember your "supervisor" (who is nothing to do with your boss at work) is making note of every time you show gratitude for your daily activity. The more good things that are noted down, the sooner you will be promoted.

4. Just before you go to bed tonight, hold your Gratitude Rock in your hand, and say the words, thank you, for the best thing that happened during the day.

DAY 10
WAY OUT OF NEGATIVITY

"An entire sea of water can't sink a ship unless it gets inside the ship. Similarly, the negativity of the world can't put you down unless you allow it to get inside you."
—Goi Nasu

The opposite of being grateful is taking things for granted. And it leads only to trouble. As far back as the Day 1 task, I asked you to focus your mindset on good things even in negative situations. Every complaint and negative thought takes you away from the great things you deserve in life. Unintentionally sometimes we take things for granted and forget to have a grateful mindset.

Entertaining negative thoughts like being jealous of another's success has the same effect. Negativity is a dreadful thing. Don't let it be your downfall.

The grateful mind is always focused on the best, this best feeling in our mind becomes our faith and this faithful gratitude feeling goes out into the universe to bring the best to us. Many people make their life unintentionally difficult when they face criticism by family members, relatives, friends. Remember: your mindset is your responsibility and you must not allow others' opinions to destroy your dream. Frustration and criticism are positive things because they can be the catalyst for change – if you let them[59]. When you encounter failure or a negative situation, don't wallow in self-pity. Start thinking about how to overcome it. Every failure brings with it the seed of an

WAY OUT OF NEGATIVITY

equivalent advantage[60]. Train your mind to see hidden opportunities in a negative situation.

Your life is in your hands, but you must learn to gain control of your thoughts. All of your problems of fear, failure, and doubts are because your MIND is ruling you. Your mind has taken over and you are the slave and victim of uncontrolled negative thoughts[61]. Every day, bit by bit, watch your thoughts. When a negative thought comes, stamp it out. Refuse to allow it to take root in you by thinking of something good instead. Think more and more good thoughts, and soon they will come automatically. You have to change your mindset towards negative situations to find the things to be grateful for in a negative situation. It is impossible to have a bad life experience with a mind full of gratitude. Gratitude helps you to eliminate negative situations. Now you know the power of a mindset full of gratitude. Every negative situation in your life will disappear like a puff of smoke.

"Abandon all negativity whatsoever, abide in deeds that are wholesome to perfectly conquer one's own mind."
—Gautama Buddha

Remember you are your biggest supporter so just focus on the good in your life even in adverse situations. Your thoughts, actions, and speaking should all be optimistic to live a wonderful life. Today's practice is finding ten things to be thankful for if you are in a negative situation. Yes, it's challenging, but it is very important for you to develop an optimistic mindset. Here is an example of finding a good thing in a bad situation – in this case, being out of work[62]:

1. I am so grateful that my life has given me spare time to do something better.
2. I am so grateful to have had more time for my love.

THE MINDSET

3. I am grateful for my past job experience which made me a better person.
4. I am truly grateful that this is the first and last time I am unemployed.
5. I am grateful for the opportunity to apply for better jobs.
6. I am grateful for all the rejection interview experiences because they are taking me closer to my dream job.
7. I am grateful for my healthy body and mind which are preparing me to excel in my next job.
8. I am grateful for the support of all the people who are helping me to make ends meet during this time of unemployment.
9. I am grateful for the rest I've had because it is preparing me to do an excellent job in the near future.
10. I am grateful for losing my job because I have learned the value of work, and having a job in my life.

An affirmative thought is 100 times more powerful than a negative one. Gratitude helps you to develop an optimistic mindset which builds more confidence in you to overcome any situation. All you have to do is practice more gratitude to develop an optimistic mindset and your life will change magically.

You will feel your gratitude is working when you are so full of gratitude you have a joyful lifting feeling in your heart. You will know the situation is about to change for the better and solutions will begin to appear in front of you. To overcome any negative situation, focus on good things about it and generate joy and happiness inside your heart; the happy heart inside will change your outside world to have better things in your life to be thankful for. Make sure you start your sentence with grateful, thankful or I am glad that..... and also write the reason why you are grateful for.

I am so happy and grateful for the spare time I have because I can learn something better to shape up my future.

I am glad that I am jobless because I have understood the value of work in my life.

Once you finish listing your 10 things then in bold letters write "Thank you, thank you, thank you for the perfect solution" after each line and read aloud your full list again.

As said on the 1st day, negative thoughts are harmful and so are the negative words. Try not to speak, think, or feel bad about anything. It is challenging but the more you practice gratitude the more you will develop an affirmative mindset. Try to get rid of all traces of negativity.

Remember in future if you find yourself in any negative situation then come back to this chapter and practice it over and over again till you start feeling joy and your mindset is filled with gratitude. Then you will have the solution.

THE MINDSET

DAY 10 TASKS

1. Repeat steps one to three of Day 4's task. Count your blessings: Make a list of ten blessings. Write why you're grateful. Reread your list, and at the end of each blessing say thank you, thank you, thank you, and feel as grateful for that blessing as you can.

2. Choose one problem or negative situation in your life that you most want to change.

3. List ten good things about that negative situation.

4. At the end of every sentence write Thank you, thank you, thank you for the prefect solution.

5. From today onwards, watch your words, thoughts and feelings. Any time you detect even a trace of negativity within you, try to get rid of it and develop an affirmative mindset.

6. Before going to bed, hold your gratitude rock in your hand and say the words thank you, thank you, thank you from the bottom of your heart for all the good things that happened today.

DAY 11
THE ELEMENT

"The thankful heart opens our eyes to a multitude of blessings that continually surround us."
—James E. Faust

Our ancestors used to offer food to the gods as a gesture expressing their gratitude for food and water which maintain the source of life[63]. Food is a gift to our bodies. Once your stomach is full, your brain functions well and you can easily carry out daily tasks. Food provides vital energy to all your body. So many people contribute to the food chain before it reaches you. With our fast life, it is impossible to give thanks for food – we take it granted.

Think about fasting, or going hungry due to work pressure. Carry on long enough and you can't focus on your work, you feel weak, you may faint. Now, do you realize the value of the food you eat? There is so much to be thankful for in every meal you received[64].

Let's take the example of groceries. We have such a variety of fruits, and they are available all year long. Farmers take care of them from the planting until the harvest. Then quality inspector s check it and pass it to the food processing factory to pack it well. From there it travels by plane, ship or truck so that a grocery store can stack it on shelves for you to buy and take home. So many people contributed to the sandwich, the snack or the meal you eat. Millions of people maintaining a global food chain. Be grateful. SPEAK your gratitude out loud.

THE MINDSET

Do the same for all the people involved in delivering clean water to your home and workplace and those of everyone who is important to you. Every time you wash, cook, drink, garden, wash your car and do some gardening, you are obliged to the people who joined together to bring the water to you. And the same goes for all the other utilities like gas, oil and electricity, and also for the emergency workers – firefighters, police and nurses – who keep you safe.

Without water, there would be no life on this planet. We are all alive because of the food we eat and the water we drink. Today onward you should express gratitude for the food and water you have.

Today's practice is to be grateful for everything you eat and drink, and for all the people who have contributed to getting it to you.

If you are in a group or meeting a client over lunch, it may be difficult to express gratitude for the food you eat. Do it later in the day. Close your eyes, think about the moment you had that meal, and say, "Thank you." The more deeply you start expressing gratitude for the small things in your life like food and water, the sooner your mindset will generate overall joy inside you and more things will show up in your life to be grateful for[65].

DAY 11 TASKS

1. Count your blessings: Make a list of ten blessings. Write why you're grateful for each. Reread your list, and at the end of each blessing say thank you, thank you, thank you, and feel as grateful for that blessing as you can.

2. Today before you eat or drink anything takes a moment to look at what you are going to eat or drink. Say thank you to all the people who have contributed to bring this food to you. Say aloud or in your mind "THANK YOU FOR THIS DELICIOUS FOOD WHICH PROVIDES NOURISHMENT TO MY BODY." OR "THANK YOU FOR THIS FOOD WHICH KEEPS ME HEALTHY AND ACTIVE."

3. If you cannot express gratitude before you eat than close your mind and go back into that moment later and repeat above sentence to yourself.

4. Be mindful about your words, thoughts and feeling. Try to get rid of any negativity within you to develop an affirmative mindset.

5. Before going to bed, hold your gratitude rock in your hand and say the words thank you, thank you, thank you from the bottom of your heart for all the good things happened today.

DAY 12
FOUNDATION OF ABUNDANCE MINDSET

*"Abundance is not something we acquire;
it is something we tune into."*
—Wayne Dyer.

So far, you have learned the immense importance of having a grateful mindset for all the good things in your life that you may previously have taken for granted. The golden rule is, "gratitude is riches and complaints are poverty." The more grateful the mindset you develop for what you have in your life at present, the sooner you will have more as your situation changes to life's natural abundance.

Anyone who complains about money will attract more situations with in adequate money, and they will have less. Their mind is continuously focused on the things they cannot afford rather than counting the things they already have in their lives. As, we learned earlier, bad feelings about money will not make you rich. You have to change your mindset towards money and then only abundance will be possible in your life. Today you are going to learn the biggest secret of the century which was always there but misunderstood by many people. The following passage from the Gospel of Matthew in the holy scriptures;

> "Whoever has will be given more, and he will
> have an abundance. Whoever does not have,
> even what he has will be taken from him."

Those words are really confusing but they apply to all your desires, relationships, love, money, health, work. Let's try to understand what they really mean.

> "Whoever has (gratitude) will be given more, and he will
> have an abundance. Whoever does not have (Gratitude),
> even what he has will be taken from him."[66]

Now this makes sense and if you put gratitude for money then it becomes:

> "Whoever has gratitude for money will be given more, and
> he will have an abundance. Whoever does not have gratitude for money, even what he has will be taken from him."

Now, this makes it very clear that one must have gratitude towards money to attract more money in their lives. I know it is challenging to feel good about money when you are struggling to pay bills. Complaining about the bill will set your mind on the frequency of receiving more bills to pay. To reverse this process, you have to think about the services you have received because of those bills.

1) **Rent**: if you are struggling to pay your rent on time, express your gratitude that you have a home to live in. Your landlord is giving you time to pay the rent. Be grateful.
2) **Utility bills**: Think about the water you use for bathing, cooking, and cleaning your house. Every time you open a tap you know water is going to flow from it. You don't need to save water because it is supplied to you easily in your home. Be grateful for

THE MINDSET

electricity because it powers your phone, light, and TV. You are able to see at night because of lamplight. Be grateful for WI-FI because you are able to reach out to anyone in almost any country. Be grateful for the utilities that make your life comfortable.

3) **Phone Services**: Be grateful for the phone bill because it means you are able to communicate with your loved ones, to check social media and to update your knowledge, all with a single click.

Be grateful for all the people who have contributed to deliver those services to you. Nothing comes free, and everything costs money to produce and deliver it.

Today's practice is about reversing your mindset about a lack of money. Gratitude is riches, complaints are poverty[67]. And remember the Gospel teaching. To change your mindset and how you feel about money is very simple. Take any bills you have due at this moment. If you have the money, then write on the top of each bill Thank you- Paid. If you do not have the money, then write on the bill "THANK YOU FOR THE MONEY." Close your eyes and think about the services, products you enjoyed using because of those who billed you. This was the first part of the practice. To set an abundance mindset find at least ten bills which you have paid in the past. On top of each bill write word THANK YOU- PAID. Close your eyes and be grateful that you had money to pay off those bills.

A famous Japanese teaching to set your mindset for abundance money is known as, "Arigato Money," or "Thank you Money."[68] Japanese people say in their mind "Arigato Money" every time they purchase, sell, donate, or pay bills. They are expressing their gratitude for the money. Ken Honda in his book, "Happy Money" explained that you should be thankful every time you use your money to buy, sell, pay off bills, and donate. You are thanking money because you are able to live a good life and help needy people. This will increase the flow of money in your life. Your mindset will generate the feelings of abundance that you have the money and it will show up in your life in reality.

Remember money will show up for you in different ways. It may be a discount, stuff given to you as a gift, installment plans for paying off bills in small amounts. It is not necessarily in the form of hard cash.

If you are paying bills or receiving bills online then just forward those bills to your personal email and save as PDF on your computer. For example, you paid your electricity bill online; now forward it to yourself and save it as PDF "Electricity Bill – Thank you- Paid." If you do not have the money to pay that bill than save it as "Electricity Bill – THANK YOU FOR MONEY AND THE GREAT SERVICE".

Today onwards don't forget to write "THANK YOU -PAID" on all the bills you pay off on time. Even if you don't have money to pay off a bill then write, "THANK YOU FOR MONEY AND THE GREAT SERVICE." We are building a mindset to be grateful for everything we have, and this will help us to develop an optimistic life for abundance success. Make this is your daily habit for each bill you pay off or receive.

Feeling grateful for paying off bills on time will increase the flow of money into your life. It is a foundation for wealth creation. A mind filled with gratitude is attached to the abundance power of the universe which returns your good feelings back to you tenfold. This law also works for bad feelings so be mindful of how you feel about money. What you give will return to you for sure.

You have to be grateful for your current money situation and play a game of wealth in your mind so your mindset will start feeling good about money. You have to build a mindset that says there is plenty for everyone. Abundance is unlimited. Whenever you feel bad about money or want to complain about money say (ideally out loud), "I have more than enough." "There is an abundance of money and it's on its way to me." I am a money magnet." "I love money and money loves me." "I am receiving money every day." "Thank you. Thank you. Thank you."

THE MINDSET

DAY 12 TASKS

1. Count your blessings: Make a list of ten blessings. Write why you're grateful for each. Reread your list, and at the end of each blessing say thank you, thank you, thank you, and feel as grateful for that blessing as you can.

2. Take any unpaid current bills you have, express gratitude for those services deeply and write "THANK YOU FOR MONEY AND THE GREAT SERVICE". Feel grateful for the amount of the bill.

3. Take at least ten bills you've paid in the past and write across the front top of each bill "THANK YOU-PAID." Feel grateful for the money you had to pay off those bills.

4. Today onwards make it your habit to write Thank You on each bill you pay and be grateful for it. If you don't have money, then use step 2 above.

5. Be mindful about your words, thoughts and feeling. Try to get rid of any negativity within you to develop an affirmative mindset.

6. Before going to bed, hold your gratitude rock in your hand and say the words thank you, thank you, thank you from the bottom of your heart for all the good things that happened today.

BE A MONEY MAGNET IN YOUR MINDSET TO ATTRACT MORE MONEY INTO YOUR LIFE.

DAY 13
POWER OF IMAGINATION

"The power of imagination makes us infinite."
—John Muir

When our conscious mind truly believes in something, it becomes reality. In history there are a number of examples of people who held a vision and imagined a particular thing as a reality in their mind, and they brought it to reality, and we call them inventors. Thomas Edison saw a clear image in his mind more than a thousand times of what a light bulb would look like. His mindset was focused on that image and provided him with the resources to make his imagination real. Whatever images are held in our minds come into reality. Our mind has the ability to create reality through imagination. Fear, sadness, and envy, each emotion begins as an external stimulus and then your mind convinces you it's real and you give up. We are in the process of reversing this. Your mind must hold an image of how you want your future life to be, and you must give a heartfelt sincere thank you for that life in your mind well in advance.

Thoughts are basic ideas which, when they ignite in our mind, become creative images, which we call ideas[69]. The idea is the beginning point of all fortunes. The emotional content of the image in our mind feeds our consciousness and provokes us into right action. The mind has infinite power to influence us. We act on the images we hold true in our mind. The inner images forecast in our mind is stimulating our actions and attitudes. If we imagine ourselves as strong, we eventually become strong. If we imagine ourselves as endowed with power, we eventually achieve ascendancy over circumstances[70]. The stronger the image of a positive scenario you hold in your mind, the more positive your action becomes to overcome the situation.

If you have doubt and fear in your mind, it casts a pall of indecision over everything[71]. We must close our minds to doubt and fear and focus on positive images. We are the creators of life though our power of imagination. If you really want to master the power of imagination you have to hold a strong image in your mind and express heartfelt gratitude for it well in advance. We do not change the people and situation around us, but we first change your perception about those people and that situation in our mind and automatically it will appear in reality. How do you know your power of imagination is working? Because you start feeling happy about the negative situation in your life as soon as your subconscious mind knows that solution is coming soon. Each of us is gifted with the power of imagination and it has infinite potential.

Nikola Tesla held a clear image of an electric power motor image in his mind. He did thousands of trials to turn his image into reality. He finally succeeded and today Tesla is the number one energy-efficient car in the world. You have to start small. Take any negative situation or relationship in your life, and imagine the best possible outcome. You won't get there immediately. You have to repeat that image many times in your mind with closed eyes and give heartful thanks for things that happen in the good ways you imagine in your mind.

If you don't like your job imagine the job you really want and say thank you. If you want to improve your relationship with a friend or colleague, imagine that person talking to you in the way you want and the two of you doing well together. Every time you use the power of imagination it generates a positive frequency around you. You can call it the law of attraction, the universe, infinite intelligence or anything else you like, but it helps you to convert that image into a

POWER OF IMAGINATION

strong thought. Your subconscious mind holds it as true and these thoughts create a vibrating frequency. This vibration of one mind is sent out into the universe and received into the mind of others. This is a way an individual's thoughts "tune in to," or communicate with the subconscious minds of others.

Today, take at least three situations or people in your life you want to change and develop a clear image of your desired end result in your mind. Repeat it as many times as possible and say thank you, thank you, thank you. If you find it difficult then write down every single detail about the desired situation or person and read it multiple times, saying thank you, thank you, thank you after each reading. There is a truth deep down inside you that has been waiting for you to discover it, and that truth is that whatever you imagine will come into reality and you deserve all the good things life has to offer[72].

THE MINDSET

DAY 13 TASKS

1. Count your blessings: Make a list of ten blessings. Write why you're grateful for each. Reread your list, and at the end of each blessing say thank you, thank you, thank you, and feel as grateful for that blessing as you can.

2. Take any current negative situation, relationship and imagine the best possible outcome of it in your favor. Say the word thank you as if that happened in your life.

3. From today onwards, if you come across any negative situation or incident in your life then imagine in your mind the best possible outcome which makes you happy and say thank you.

4. Be mindful about your words, thoughts and feelings. Try to get rid of any negativity within you to develop an affirmative mindset.

5. Think about any negative scenario that happened today, imagine an affirmative image of it in your mind and say thank you.

6. Before going to bed, hold your gratitude rock in your hand and say the words thank you, thank you, thank you for the best things that happened during the day.

7. Read tomorrows practice today because it starts when you wake up.

The more you master this practice the happier you will feel, and your mindset will change for the better.

DAY 14
GOOD MORNING

"Write in your heart that every day is the best day in the year."
—Ralph Waldo Emerson

Every morning is a blessing for you to do better things for yourself and others. How lucky you are to be waking up healthy again to see this world and explore its beauty. Say to yourself: "I am grateful to be alive and this new day will be filled with an exciting opportunity." Our mindset is happy when we live in the present moment and the present is every beautiful morning you get. We are preparing our minds to be happy and full of joy in the morning so that all through the day we can do better things. Let's count how many things you use in the morning to makes your life easy. If you slept on a bed, that would be a luxury for a homeless person, would it not?[73] You use toothpaste, brush, hot water, mirror, towel, cloths, soap, shampoo, perfume, clean clothes. So many people contributed to making all these things for you to use. Say thank you for all these amenities you have in your life. You have breakfast to eat and a kitchen that contains what you need. Not necessarily – yet – all you want, but all you need. Your morning is off to an excellent start.

Think about people who don't have all these things. Express your gratitude for each small thing you use to make your morning comfortable. The more gratitude you will have, the more your mindset will fill with happiness and you will start each day with joy. Things may happen later in the day which affect your affirmative mindset

THE MINDSET

but when you start your day with a happy mindset the day will become happier and all the best events will line up.

If you feel each day or morning is not important then try to run your day without your morning routine. Make a habit of starting your day with affirmative thoughts and a happy mindset[74]. That is the most important time of the day when you can harm your mindset with negative thoughts. You can practice meditation for ten minutes to calm your mind. You are practicing gratitude rock before going to bed every day. You go to sleep with a happy mindset and you should maintain the same state of mind when you wake up in the morning. **If your morning routine includes reading a newspaper or watching the news while having your breakfast, then you should stop doing that until you complete all practices in this book.** There is hardly any good news in the newspaper or on TV, and it will affect your calm and happy mindset. Instead, listen to your favorite song. There is no way a negative thought can enter into your mind when it is focused on finding a good thing to be grateful for.

Count all the good things in the morning which make you happy. Express your gratitude for all these small things when you start your morning. Think about the people who made your morning happy even though you and they will never meet. Be grateful for your morning routine that makes your morning enjoyable and gives you energy for the day. A happy mind attracts happier events to be grateful for in the day. Try to make each day the best day of the year.

You learned the power of imagination in the previous chapter. Try to apply it to your everyday schedule. Have in your mind a clear image of the events you want to happen or take place to make you happy. Say thank you for the happy day well in advance. Since the day I have understood the power of the gratitude mindset, I have never woken up with aches or bad feelings. I wake with excitement and have a clear picture in my mind of how my day will unfold and I express my gratitude. When I feel happy, I become a magnet for happy and joyful events in my life. One good thing after another lines up and my day feels like a magical fairy tale. The more good things happen, the more grateful I become and my mindset multiplies the good experience in my life.

DAY 14 TASKS

1. As soon as you open your eyes in the morning say it loud or in your mind, "I AM GRATEFUL TO BE ALIVE IN A NEW DAY FILLED WITH AN EXCITING OPPORTUNITY."
2. Say thank you and express your gratitude for the things you use as you get ready to start your day.
3. Count your blessings: Make a list of ten blessings. Write why you're grateful for each of them. Reread your list, and at the end of each blessing say thank you, thank you, thank you, and feel as grateful for that blessing as you can.
4. Before you leave for work or start your day, imagine all events well in advance to make you happy and say, "Thank for my day having gone well!"
5. Before going to bed, hold your gratitude rock in your hand and say the words thank you, thank you, thank you for the best things that happened during the day.

DAY 15
THE PEOPLE

---

*We must find time to stop and thank the people
who make a difference in our lives.*
—John F. Kennedy

Showing gratitude is one of the most powerful things humans can do for each other. From the day we are born we received support, love, and guidance from our parents, from close family members, but also from many people who help us to live a day to day routine life. Those who made a big difference in our life through their guidance, support, and help are the most memorable ones[75]. The motivational friend, a colleague, a supervisor who touched your life at different levels and contributed to the great life you are living today.

Today you are going to look back at your life and find people who helped you and made a difference in your life. It is possible that those people are no longer with you but you can still have their memories in your mind. Today your mindset will focus on being grateful for all the people whose guidance, support, love and motivation changed the stream of your life. Whenever you think about that person you should feel grateful that you meet that person.

"Let us be grateful to the people who make us happy, they are
the charming gardeners who make our souls blossom."
—Marcel Proust

THE MINDSET

The person may have been a family member, close friend, friends of friends, the one who introduced you to your spouse, a professional who helped you like a doctor, nurse or therapist –it can be anyone. In our life, we come across so many people, and they may change our life dramatically or just be there to make us feel happy[76]. Some of my friends are younger than me and some are older but, all the same, I have learned so many things in my life from my friends. I give thanks every time I think about the amazing people I've known and I feel happy about the way they have changed the course of my life.

Once I was at home, trying to learn to knit. I'm left-handed. My art teacher has more than a decade of experience in crochet, but she is right-handed. I give up on crochet because I couldn't hold the needle in my right hand. Somehow my teacher found a left-handed student who had learned crochet from her grandmother and that girl, who was three years younger than me, taught me how to crochet with my left hand. Today, thanks to her, I can crochet a sweater or scarf to keep myself warm in chilly Boston weather. It really doesn't matter who she was, or how old; when I needed someone to teach me to knit, she was there. That's how the Universe works. Today I am not in touch with her nor I can find her to express my gratitude but, in my mind, I thank her for teaching me to crochet whenever I knit something new. I learned the art of gratitude late in my life – but I learned it. And so must you.

Today, find time to go to some quiet place with your gratitude book and think about the three most important people who made a big difference in your life. It doesn't matter whether they are alive today or around you. You have their memories in your mind that's all you need to continue this practice. Take one person at a time and, say out loud as if they were in front of you and it's your chance to express your gratitude towards them, say "THANK YOU" to them and tell them what you are thankful for. Don't say more than five to six lines at most but feel the happiness you generate while expressing gratitude.

You should do this practice for all three people at once because it will help you to generate deeper gratitude and your heart will be filled with happiness at the end of this practice. Once your mindset starts focusing on gratitude it is easier to retain it for the next person. If you practice it at different times then your mindset will not be in the deeper state each time.

Here is an example of what you can say:

Dear Noopur, thank you for supporting me during my professional career. I was very impatient, but you consoled me and helped me to be patient. Because of your kind words, I became a humble and polite person. I learned from you that we should only focus on good things in others and ignore bad things. You taught me the real meaning of the proverb, "An eye for an eye will leave the whole world blind" said by Mahatma Gandhi. Thank you, Noopur!

If you are not in a position to say it aloud then just write in your gratitude book as if you were writing a letter to that person. Once you are done with it, list ten people who made a difference in your day to day life. It can be a parent, grandparent, aunt, uncle, friend, sibling, employer, employee. Write the reason you are grateful to them, and write Thank you after you finish the sentence.

Examples:

1. Thank you, Petya, for always helping me to find a solution during my difficult time. Thank you, thank you, thank you!
2. Thank you, Diana, for bringing Rocky to visit me often because Rocky gave me the joy of having a pet for a while. Thank you, thank you, thank you!

Once you are done with this practice you will feel happy. Happiness is the cause of an affirmative mindset[77]. When you have a positive mindset, you attract more reasons to be happy in the real world. The more joy you feel in your life, the more optimistic experiences will be attracted to you. You will become a magnet of happiness. The joy within you will create a good vibe or frequency around you to attract more wonderful things in your life. This is the magic of your mindset and it is very simple to achieve. You will start noticing how things are changing around you that tell you your gratitude mindset is working correctly.

DAY 15 TASKS

1. Count your blessings: Make a list of ten blessings. Write why you're grateful about each. Reread your list, and at the end of each blessing say thank you, thank you, thank you, and feel as grateful for that blessing as you can.
2. Find three important people who made a difference in your life and either express your gratitude out loud or write them a letter. Don't fail to say why you are grateful to them.
3. Make a list of ten people who helped you to have a comfortable day to day routine life and thank them.
4. Before going to bed, hold your gratitude rock in your hand and say the words thank you, thank you, thank you for the best things that happened during the day.

With these fifteen days of practice, you have built on all the past things that happened in your life a foundation to shape who you are today. From tomorrow onwards, you will practice using mind power to change things in your day to day life.

DAY 16
MIRACLES HAPPEN OVERNIGHT

"Imagination is more important than knowledge. Knowledge is limited. Imagination encircles the world."
—Albert Einstein

You have learned the power of imagination in a previous chapter. With practice, you have developed a grateful mindset for the things you had in the past and the things you have right now. It's time to use the power of your mindset to make your future dreams and desires come true[78]. On day one you were asked to make a list of dreams you want to achieve. If you didn't do it then, you really do need to make one now, because today you are going to use gratitude for your dreams and desire. Your mindset should be focused on your dreams and you should trust that they will be manifested.

How do miracles happen overnight? It is very simple when your mindset holds a clear image of desire and you express gratitude for it well in advance, it will manifest. If you recall the chapter gratitude is life. Egyptians used to perform rituals to express their thanks for food well in advance. The best way is to express gratitude before your desire comes true and then it will happen. It is very common in many cultures to develop a gratitude mindset for desires and wishes before they come true.

According to the law of the universe, like attracts like. If your mindset is focused on a clear image of the desire you want to manifest, it will create vibrations around you and the universe will conspire to bring it to you. Look at your dreams list and go through it. You have to be very specific about what you want. You must have a very firm image in your mind of what it looks like and how happy you will feel after receiving it, but your mindset should be feeling happy as if it is already yours[79]. As if it has already happened and you are expressing gratitude for it. In your mindset, hold a clear picture that it is already yours and you are living your dream life. The happier your mindset is, the sooner what you want will manifest in your life.

Gratitude is a power of your mindset. It is something you have deep inside you. It is the strongest feeling that generates an affirmative mindset. Every one of us says thank you or feels grateful once the desire is manifested. If it does not happen the way you want, your gratitude mindset is not focused. Whatever you want in your life you must be grateful for it before you have it as well as when you actually receive it. Applying gratitude for the desire before you receive it creates a clear image of it in your mind. Your mind becomes the magnet for that desire and you have done almost 80% of what is needed to achieve your desire.

When you go to a restaurant and order food, you are relaxed because you know it is going to be served to you soon. You don't obsess over what the cook is going to use or how he is going to cook it. None of that is your job. You are just enjoying the waiting by feeling the taste of that food in your mindset and you feel happy about it. How your desire is going to manifest is not your job. Your job is to know that it *will* manifest, and to feel grateful for it *before the event*. If you want $100, don't think about the cash appearing in your hand. It can be some type of gift you really need worth $100. It can be a credit note, it can be a discount, it can be someone giving it to you, you might discover money you have forgotten or money someone owes you. Your job is to clearly imagine in your mind that you already have $100 and express your gratitude for it. Play games in your mind what you are going to do with it and express the gratitude that you have the money beforehand. Then the $100 will be there.

THE MINDSET

Now look at the desires you listed earlier and choose one. Write down every single detail of it and hold a clear image of it in your mind as if it's already yours[80]. Sit down with your gratitude book and create a separate list of the top ten desires you want to manifest as though you have already received them. Thank you, thank you, thank you for_____, and fill in the blank with your dream, desire, wish.

Let's look at few examples as follows:

Thank you, thank you, thank you for the clear medical report that shows I am perfectly healthy!

Thank you, thank you, thank you for the money!

Thank you, thank you, thank you for the foreign trip!

Thank you, thank you, thank you for the car at discounted price!

Thank you, thank you, thank you for the perfect life partner!

Writing a thank you three times in a row focuses your mindset towards more gratitude. The number three is considered a mystical number associated with creation[81]. Three wise men, three wishes, three guesses. Number three is also associated with creation: in many holy books, God's three greatest creations are Heaven, Earth, and the abyss. Hence, it is very important to write three times in a row THANK YOU!

Once, you are done with this practice, you have to train your mind to focus on satisfying your desire. To do so, go through your list of desires one at a time and answer the following questions in your mind with a clear image:

1. How happy are you feeling to have your dream come true?
2. Who will you tell about your desire and what medium will you use (In-person, on a call, in-text message, in an email or mail)?
3. What was the first thing you did after receiving your desire?

Add each and every detail in simple words which will help you to form a clear image in your mind. Hold on to that image and be grateful well in advance for the desire you have received.

To practice this regularly, you can have a visualization board or miracle board. Put a photoshopped picture there of the places you want to visit with you in it. Put a photo of you with your dream car and imagine taking a long drive in it. Put the list of your top ten desires on it and read it aloud and imagine it clearly in your mind. Put this miracle board somewhere you can see every day. If your desire comes true, replace it with another one. Write a Thank you three times on the photo or tick the list once it is manifested. You have to believe in your mind that everything is possible, and miracles do happen overnight if you have a grateful heart.

DAY 16 TASKS

1. Count your blessings: Make a list of ten blessings. Write why you're grateful for each one. Reread your list and at the end of each blessing say thank you, thank you, thank you, and feel as grateful for that blessing as you can.

2. Make a list of ten desires, wishes, dreams which are very important to you. Write down your list as: Thank you, thank you, thank you for ....

3. After completing your list, go through each wish again and with closed eyes have the feeling that you already received it and answer the following questions with a clear image in your mind.

    3.1   How happy are you feeling to have your dream come true?

    3.2   Who will you tell about your desire and what medium you will use?

    3.3   What was the first thing you did after receiving your desire?

4. Before going to bed, hold your gratitude rock in your hand and say the words thank you, thank you, thank you from the bottom of your heart for the best things that happened during the day.

DAY 17
EVERY DAY IS A BLESSING

"Intentions compressed into words enfold magical power."
—Deepak Chopra

To make each day magnificent, it is very important to give thanks well in advance before you start your day. In the previous chapter, you have learned the importance of having a gratitude mindset before you receive as well as after you receive. It is a very simple thing to do and hardly takes a few minutes. This small change in mindset will bring a drastic change in your day. Like attracts like is the law of the universe and you must follow the same law by clearly imagining the day before you live it! Fill your mindset for the great day you have before you have it. As we all follow some schedule in our life each day, imagine every task you are going to do on that day is done right and say thank you for it. The more your mindset creates these grateful frequencies, the more the universe will return good experiences to you.

If you think you don't have the power to change your day well in advance, just think back to a day when you woke up in a bad mood. Your mindset created a bad feeling about the day in your heart and one by one thing got worse until, by the end of the day, you were exhausted[82].

You are doing a gratitude rock practice every night to ensure that you fall asleep with a happy mindset and joyful heart. Waking up in a bad mood happens because, intentionally or unintentionally, you went to sleep thinking about something negative[83]. Gratitude rock practice before going to bed and counting your blessings early in the morning guarantees that your mindset is always on happy, joyful, and affirmative frequencies.

Have a grateful heart for everything you have and everything you are going to have is the simplest thing ever. It will fill your mind with feelings of joy. You become a magnet of joy and attract more good things[84]. To have a wonderful day you should feel good and maintain that good mindset throughout the day.

In today's world, we all have a daily planner, schedule, calendar or to-do list that makes it easy for us to follow the day. Whether it is a small task or a big task you must have a good mindset before you begin it. If you have your to-do list then read each item on your list well in advance and clearly imagine in your mind that it has been done and went well, and the outcome made you feel good.

When you intentionally plan your day well in advance, all the hurdles and struggles will be moved out of your way. I have experienced it many times since I have set a grateful mindset. The more you give gratitude well in advance, the easier and smoother your day will become. You will start feeling that every day is a blessing and a wonderful day in your life. A task will not feel like a burden, but you will enjoy it as it will become easy with your mindset power.

It will take only a few minutes to practice gratitude well in advance for your day. You can do it while brushing, bathing or getting dressed for the day. Go through each task in your mind and hold a clear picture of it. Whether it is driving to work, getting a seat in the subway, finding a parking spot, a meeting, a presentation, a call with a client, a deal you are going to make. Plan the outcome of every task and routine in your mindset clearly from the start of the morning, the afternoon, and the evening till the day is ending. Imagine you are saying thank you for the task that has gone well for the excellent day at night. If you are working as a cashier, server, waitress, or at the store where your day is unpredictable then say, "THANK YOU FOR MY DAY HAVING GONE WELL AND ALL THE GREAT NEWS COMING TO ME TODAY!"[85]

Let's look at few examples of routine work as follows:

1. Thank you for the easy drive to work.
2. Thank you for the parking spot.
3. Thank you for the less crowded subway or bus.
4. Thank you for the excellent outcome of the meeting.
5. Thank you for the easy cleaning day.
6. Thank you for the easy and smooth travel experience.
7. Thank you for the productive day at work.
8. Thank you for the amazing energy from the workout session.

If possible, try to say this aloud. If you are not in a situation to say it out loud, say it in your head. Remember to imagine a clear picture of the outcome in your mind. The more you practice it, the more you will master it to have a blessed day every day.

DAY 17 TASKS

1. Count your blessings: Make a list of ten blessings. Write why you're grateful for each one. Reread your list, and at the end of each blessing say thank you, thank you, thank you, and feel as grateful for that blessing as you can.
2. In the morning, go through your day plan or to do list, imagine the clearly affirmative outcome of each item and say thank you and express your gratitude in your mindset.
3. Once you are done with the day's plan, say "Thank you for my day having gone well, and all the great news coming to me today."
4. Before going to bed, hold your gratitude rock in your hand and say the words thank you, thank you, thank you from the bottom of your heart for the best things that happened during the day.

DAY 18
HEAL YOUR RELATIONSHIPS

"A grateful heart is a magnet for Miracles."
—Unknown

We all at some point in our life have difficulty in a relationship or have to deal with a broken relationship. It is hard to get back to normal. Our mindset is harmed because of those relationships. In our minds, whenever we look back at those memories some of them bring a smile to our face. Blame, grudge, anger or a broken heart can be healed easily. Your mind has the ability to use a power of gratitude to turn any broken relationship, blame or anger into a pleasant and harmonious relationship. Our mind is gifted with resilience to keep ourselves from being carried away by negative emotions[86].

The power of gratitude can improve any difficult relationship. When we start with a relationship, we look for the best qualities in another person but, with time, our ability to see the best in another person slows down and then we start blaming, complaining about the relationship. We stop being grateful and look for faults to blame another person. Blaming and complaining about the problem in a relationship is never going to improve it; it will make it worse and ultimately affect your life. Whether it is a current or a past relationship which filled your mindset with bad feelings for another person, it is important to get rid of those negative, bad emotions from your mindset to clear it for the better life ahead.

THE MINDSET

> *"Holding on to anger is like grasping a hot coal with the intent of throwing it at someone else; you are the one who gets burned."*
> —*Gautama Buddha*

A heart filled with gratitude will help you to remove bad emotions from your mind to live a better life!

Broken marriage? Taking care of your children after divorce? Look at your kids. Without your ex-partner, they wouldn't be there. Your ex helped make your children and that is the greatest creation of all. Express your gratitude to your ex-partner for giving you children. Never say bad things about your ex to your children and you will teach them the best way to live. It's your relationship that broke and not your child's, so don't fill the child's mind with bad emotions about marriage. Instead, teach them gratitude to develop their mindset to look at every relationship with a grateful heart. It will help your kids to have a harmonious relationship. If your relationship is going through a bad time, it should not be obvious to your children so that they don't develop negative emotions and may develop a mindset that does not pursue success in their own relationships.

If your heart is breaking over the death of your dear one, look at the great times you had together. Be thankful that their presence made your life feel great. And there's the bittersweet pleasure of knowing you now have time for other activities you couldn't do when you were responsible for another person. You can spend time on the hobbies you like the most. And, although it may not seem like that right now, maybe – maybe – one day you'll date again and have the chance of another good relationship in your life. If your child died, then look at the orphanage kids waiting for their forever homes to have a family. You have a chance to give a better life to someone who really needs it.

In today's practice, you are going to take a hurtful relationship and find the good things that happened in your life due to that relationship. The purpose of this practice is to rid yourself of grief. The greatest secret to overcoming any heartache is to have, as much as possible, a normal and natural mindset. It doesn't matter if the person is dead, is in your life right now, or is a past relationship. Sit down with your gratitude journal and list ten things to be grateful for about that person. Look back at your memories and focus your mind on the good things you got from that relationship. Go back in memory to when the relationship was good or had just started. What interested you in that person? What qualities did you like about that person? If the relationship was never good, then think about the good things you learned from that relationship to have better relationships in the future.

This practice is about healing your own mindset for the betterment of your life. Don't focus on who was wrong or right, or what that person did to you. There are good things in every relationship, and you are going to focus only on good things or qualities in that relationship. Remember you are doing this to rid your mindset of negative emotions to make it affirmative for the best life ahead. If you have more than one hurtful relationship, look at each relationship and list ten things about it until your mindset is clear of all bad emotions and feelings about that person. Here are examples of what your list will look like. Write it as if you are talking to that person. Here is an example of a mother and son relationship after the mother's death. Our relationship with our parents should never be taken for granted because there are many orphaned children who will never experience it.

1. Mom, I am grateful for all the things you did for me.
2. Mom, I am grateful for the love, care and food you gave me to be strong.
3. Mom, I am grateful for the time when you took care of me when I was ill.
4. Mom, I am grateful for your support to save me from dad's scolding.

THE MINDSET

5. Mom, I am grateful for the time when you surprised me in my sad moments with my favorite food.
6. Mom, I am grateful because you taught me the value of money by giving me chores to earn it.
7. Mom, I am grateful for the independent life I lived in the city because you taught me to cook.
8. Mom, I am grateful because you gave me money to buy my first car.
9. Mom, I am grateful for the time when I took care of you in our old house during your last days.
10. Mom, I am grateful that you rest in peace and I am free to start my world tour.

When I did my first relationship healing practice, I had a tear of joy in my eyes. It felt so good that I had something good from that relationship. I repeated this practice with a couple of relationships and at the end of each practice, I was filled with joy. My mindset was free from the burden because it was filled with gratitude and the great lessons I had from those relationships. The main purpose of this practice is to reach that point in your mind where not a single bad emotion or feeling exists. As stated at the beginning of this book, you are not to say or have a bad feeling about anyone around you or yourself. This will help your mind to develop resilience to create positive energy within you.

When you have done this practice for past relationships, your heart will be clear of hate and you will feel more happiness and peace about it. This will help your mindset to drastically bring changes into your current relationship. You will experience that quarrels are over, and you are into a harmonious relationship.

If you are using this practice for your current relationship, try not to complain at all. You will see an improvement. Putting resilience into a mindset will change your body language and others will start liking you more. Your mindset is in peace and filled with joy and you will become a magnet for a better relationship in your life.

Remember to come back to this chapter in the future if you find yourself in a challenging relationship. It can be parents, grandparents, siblings, colleagues, managers. You will remove the difficulties in that relationship and will improve the harmony in that relationship.

DAY 18 TASKS

1. Count your blessings: Make a list of ten blessings. Write why you're grateful for each one. Reread your list and at the end of each blessing say thank you, thank you, thank you, and feel as grateful for that blessing as you can.
2. Choose one relationship from the past or current relationship you want to improve.
3. In your gratitude journal make a list of ten things you are grateful about the person you have chosen. Write it down as if talking to that person. Person ------Name-----I am grateful for …..what?
4. Before going to bed, hold your gratitude rock in your hand and say the words thank you, thank you, thank you from the bottom of your heart for the best things that happened during the day.

DAY 19
HEALTH IS A GIFT

"Take care of your body. It's the only place you have to live."
—Jim Rohn

Our mindset plays a vital role in maintaining our health. Feeling healthy, energized, and happy is our natural state of mind. Many people surround themselves with illness, depression, aging, health problems, all of which is due to a lack of gratitude for the health they already have. Beauty and health depend on the state of your mind[87]. A healthy mindset will lead to a healthy body

Precisely, the thoughts and feelings you feed your mindset with result in good or bad health. Medical researchers have proved that bad feelings like resentment, hate, grudge, ill will, jealously, vindictiveness are responsible for ill health[88].

Thoughts and gratitude are the most important aspects of your mindset to maintain great health. Gratitude helps you to restore the natural flow of health in the mind and body so that you heal quickly. Our mindset is closely related to the aging of our bodies[89]. Gratitude along with medicine, nutrition, and care go hand in hand to maintain good health forever. Your mindset holds as a true fact that your body will get old and unattractive[90]. Have you seen people who do not age at all, looking young forever without any surgery? It is because they have changed their mindset towards their body repair, making it continuously newer and fresh.

THE MINDSET

There are two kinds of age: the age of your body and the age of your mind. Your physical body is the construction of today and for use today. Your mind is another growth, millions of years old. It has changed many bodies and it will go with your soul and hence mind growth is important. The older your spirit, the older your mind[91]. Many people do not feel good about their physical appearance. You can use your mindset power to preserve beauty, body shape, health, and make it look attractive. **Remember if your mind feels bad about your body it is a negative emotion which makes you ugly, unhealthy, weak, diseased, and unattractive. Whenever you feel an illness or body ache it is because your mind has unintentionally consumed negative emotions**. To get rid of those negative emotions, feed your mindset with a good feeling. Gratitude is the easiest way to do so.

"If you have health, you probably will be happy, and if you have health and happiness, you have all the wealth you need, even if it is not all you want."
—Elbert Hubbard

Do you know anyone who doesn't want health and happiness? If you do not have a good feeling about your body, the law of attraction says you will attract more complaints about your body and your health will decrease. You have to understand the vital role your feelings play in creating troubles in your body. Here is a list of five emotions and their effect on your body:

1) **ANGER** weakens your liver

2) **FEAR** weakens your kidneys

3) **GRIEF** weakens your lungs

4) **STRESS** weakens your heart

5) **WORRY** weakens your stomach

It is very important for you always to feel happy and to be happy you must have gratitude in your heart.

You may be not keeping well or may even be in a lot of pain, but you can use conscious autosuggestion to receive the gift of health. Say loudly or repeat in your mind as many times possible, "Every day, in every way, my health is getting better and better." This is a very powerful sentence. When using this affirmation, say it very slowly and with full conviction of the meaning of the words. It is the force we put into words that makes them powerful.

Your mindset and thoughts are responsible for the fine line on your face. You are everyday thinking yourself into some phase of character and facial expression, good or bad. If your thoughts are permanently cheerful, so is your mindset and hence you will have a cheerful face. If you have a peevish, quarrelsome mood this kind of mindset will put ugly lines on your face. The thought or mood of fear has tremendous impact to turn your hair gray in a few hours.

Today's practice is to increase your health and set your mindset for the abundance of health and beauty for your future.

Step 1: Health you have received (Past)

Look back at your life and the great health you had as a kid to enjoy every sport, waking up energetic every morning. Then adolescence and adult life. Recollect those good memories of healthy life and express deep gratitude for it in your mindset and say Thank you, thank you, thank you with grace and a happy feeling.

Step 2: Health you are continuing to receive (Present)

Think about your body today, with all organs, systems, and senses acting together to keep you alive. Your brain, hair, skull, eyes, skin, nose, sense of smell, mouth, tongue, throat, respiratory system, heart, lungs, stomach, bladder, kidney, arms, legs. Choose ten functions or organs in your body for good health and, one by one, mentally thank them for keeping you alive. You can say things like, "Thank you heart for purifying blood for my whole body." Or "Thank you eyes for helping me to see the beauty in everything." Your health is a gift and you should on no account take it for granted.

Step 3: Health you want to receive (Future)

Choose something about your body you want to improve like perfect weight, toned body, or more energy. Imagine a clear picture of how it looks and say thank you in advance as if you have already achieved that perfect weight or body shape. Take at least three functions of the body you want to improve and say thank you in advance while seeing in your mind a clear picture that you have already received it.

When we are diagnosed with illness, we try to collect information and unintentionally our mindset is more focused on disease, and it gets worse. At the beginning of the pandemic year 2020, I had a small rash on my right hand, and I was taking over the counter medicine for it. I kept searching every day on the internet about whether it is a food allergy, hives, medicine reaction and in 2 weeks it had spread all over my body. I was in pain and couldn't sleep at night. Rather than focusing on healing, I was watching it spreading day by day. Medicine was not working on it. Finally, I started focusing on clear skin the normal state of my skin. I used autosuggestion, "Every day, in every way my skin is getting better and better." I changed my mindset about the rash and within a week it had completely healed and never came back. When you have an illness, focus on the healthy body to change your mindset, about it. In your mind, build an ideal strong, healthy and vigorous self and make your mind a magnet to attract more health into your life.

DAY 19 TASKS

1. Count your blessings: Make a list of ten blessings. Write why you're grateful for each one. Reread your list, and at the end of each blessing say thank you, thank you, thank you, and feel as grateful for that blessing as you can.

2. Choose ten different times in your life when you felt on top of the world and give sincere thanks for the great health.

3. Think about three functions of your body that are well and one by one give thanks for each one.

4. Choose one thing about your body or health you want to improve, and spend some time visualizing yourself with the ideal state of your body or health. Give thanks for this ideal state.

5. Before going to bed hold your gratitude rock in your hand and say the words thank you, thank you, thank you from the bottom of your heart for the best things that happened during the day.

DAY 20
MONEY MAGNET MINDSET

"Abundance is already within you. Let it out."
—Laura Emily

No one is kept in poverty because of the shortness in the supply of riches; there is plenty for everyone. having no mindset or a bad mindset about money will never bring money to you. If you want to attract money, you may find that you have more power by imaging having the things you want the money for. If there is a lack of money in your life, then your feelings and beliefs about money are most likely not very good, and thinking instead about having the things money will buy may feel much better. You have to learn to decipher your feelings and choose the thoughts that feel better because that's where your power is.

The moment you have a bad thought or feeling about money you start to lose it. If you see others getting richer and you envy them then you are creating a negative emotion in your mindset about money[92]. The feeling of disappointment or envy that it's not happening to you is affecting your mindset. If someone else can get rich, so can you. Any time you hear about someone else receiving money or success, get excited as if it were happening to you because how you react to the news is everything. If you react with joy and excitement for the other person, you are saying "YES" to more money and success for yourself[93]. You have already learned about negative emotions and your mindset is day by day becoming more affirmative.

According to the law of attraction, a grateful mind eventually attracts great things to itself. If you feel good about money, you will attract situations to make money or get free or as a gift things you wanted. If you are currently having difficulty with money then you have to be grateful for the abundance and riches you are going to receive in the future. No matter what your current situation is, focus your mind on playing a wealth game. Be grateful for the wealth in advance. You can't have gratitude and bad feelings about money at the same time[94]. It is the power of gratitude that eliminates any lack of belief or bad feeling. The person who practices gratitude every day is always happy and will attract more happiness every day. When you are grateful for money you move away from any negative emotions. There is no space for a bad feeling if your mindset and heart are filled with gratitude.

You have already learned how to use gratitude to bring riches to you. You have to understand that riches can come into your life in different forms and you have to be grateful for everything which adds to your riches. It can be credit card points, a tax refund, an unexpected check from the client, a lotto win, a gift of something you intended to buy. Discount at grocery stores, the free item you received for other purchases, someone paying for your meal all save money and are equivalent to receiving a payment. You have to be grateful for each of these things. If you want to buy something and a friend or neighbor offers it to you, riches are flowing to you. Any discount is a form of wealth.

How the money comes is not your concern; what you have to do is feel grateful and focus your mindset on riches you want to achieve in your life. There are no coincidences. Everything means something. Whenever you receive something which costs money, feel grateful and hold on to that joyful feeling of having everything you want.

When I came to the USA in 2016, I was a student and living with very limited amenities. My roommates were senior and each had struggled to get an on-campus job but I got one just seven days after

THE MINDSET

my arrival. I was so grateful for it. Everyone was surprised that I got a job so quickly. People around me were very generous and helped me in so many ways. I always said thank you every time I received help and I felt in my heart that I would be capable of helping someone in the near future. I was grateful for the small amount of money I was making in that on-campus job and slowly I came across different opportunities like volunteering at a shelter (I got free food), baby sitting and pet sitting for friends of friends to get more money and somewhere to stay. I was grateful for what I had, and I was always provided with more than I needed to survive. Free food, free movie or concert tickets, a free ride home, free printing services, nice dresses donated by rich people in the area. I was living in a shared apartment and after a while I was able to rent a studio apartment for myself even in a costly city like Boston.

Today's practice is about starting to attract the money you really want. This proven method is also known as "magic check." If you have a certain amount in your mindset then you will feel better about it and it will generate joyful feelings for that money. The mindset is needed to attract one dollar just the same as to attract ten thousand dollars but, in your mindset, one dollar is easy to attract and hence you get smaller amounts easily. If, you can attract one dollar you can attract more; it's all about your mindset.

"in the magical universe there are no coincidences and no accidents. Nothing happens unless someone wills it to happen."
—William Burroughs

At the end of this chapter, you will find a blank check which you can photo-copy. Fill up this check with the amount of money you want to receive and feel grateful as if you have already received it. Think about what you are going to purchase with that amount of money and feel the joy in your heart. Remember to start with a small amount first because it will give you a fast result. Carry this check with you or keep it in a place where you can see it often. Every time you see it say thank you, thank you, thank you for the amount of money.

When I first used it, I needed fifty dollars to buy a pair of snowshoes and so I made the check out for fifty dollars. I carried it with me everywhere during the fall time and looked at it several times and then imagined the pair of shoes I am walking with. On the third day, I received an email from the school that I have been selected in a lucky draw and won a $50 voucher. I was overjoyed when I received it and was talking to my professor and asked her where I can buy good quality snowshoes. She offered me a free ride to tax-free outlets over the weekend and guess what: I got $75 worth of shoes for just $30 because she was a member of some merchandised store. I was so grateful for it and then afterwards I kept replacing the amounts in my check. Every time I received what I asked for I wrote thank you three times on the back of the check and replaced it with a new one.

From today onwards, keep your check with you or put it on your visualizing board where you can see it every day. Be grateful in advance before receiving actual money. You can do this for as long as you want.

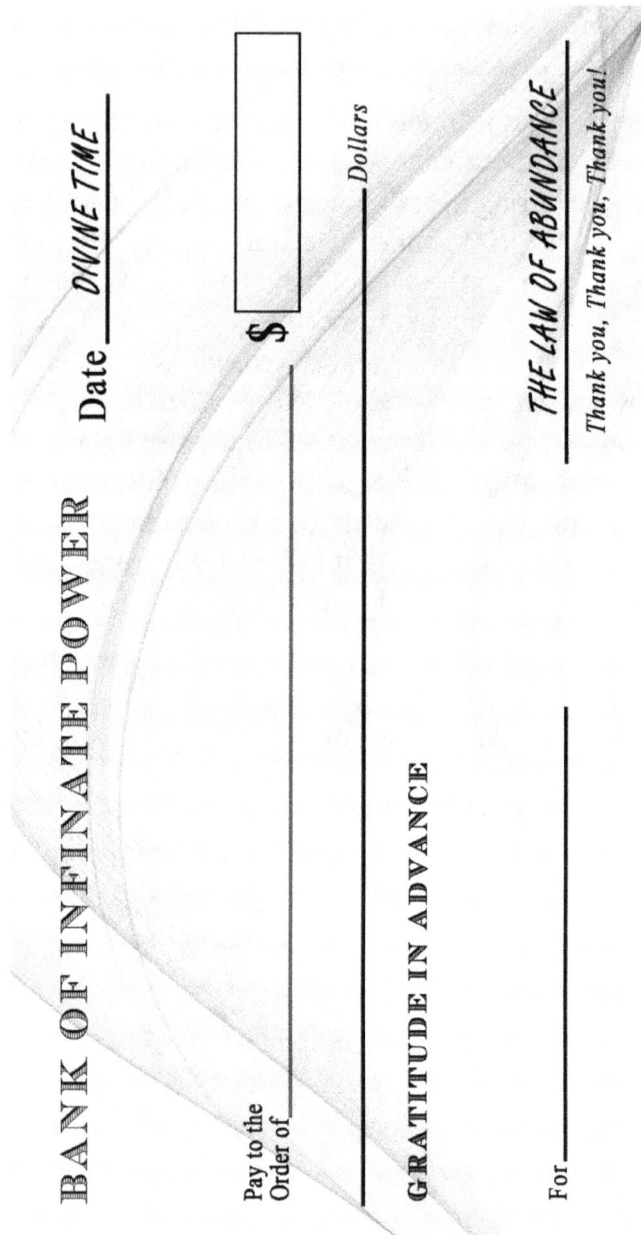

Download your own check at:
http://mindsetbymayura.com/abundancecheck/

DAY 20 TASKS

1. Count your blessings: Make a list of ten blessings. Write why you're grateful for each one. Reread your list and at the end of each blessing say thank you, thank you, thank you, and feel as grateful for that blessing as you can.

2. Fill in the mindset check with the amount of money you want to receive and all other details.

3. Hold your check in your hand and imagine a clear picture of the things you are doing after receiving that amount. Feel grateful as much you can.

4. From today onwards, try to look at your mindset check as many as times possible every day. Say thank you three times for the amount of the money you have received. "Thank you, thank you, thank you for the hundred dollars" OR "I am grateful to receive one hundred dollars."

5. Keep your check on your visualization board or in your purse or wallet where you can see it often.

6. If you manifested the thing you wish the money for then write thank you three times on the back of the check before you discard it or make a folder to save it.

7. You can use check for the same or different amounts as many times as you want.

8. Before going to bed, hold your gratitude rock in your hand and say the words thank you, thank you, thank you from the bottom of your heart for the best things that happened during the day.

DAY 21
MANIFEST YOUR DESIRE

"Keep your eyes out for magical moments, they're everywhere!
Live with passion today and every day!
—Tony Robbins

So far you have learned that you only need the right mindset to change your life. If you have a positive frame of mind, you can manifest positive things in your life. The more your heart is filled with gratitude and the clearer the image you hold in your mind about your future life, the events, situation or people will start showing up in your life to bring forth the life you want to live. The life you are living today is a thought you clearly imagined in your life in the past, isn't it?[95] You just have to be clear about your mindset to be successful. You can create magical moments in your life with just a grateful heart and an affirmative mindset.

Always remember that the things on which your mind is focused become your reality[96]. If we focus on more good feelings, happiness, and gratitude for every small moment of joy, it will bring happier moments into our life. If your mind is more focused on worry and fearful thoughts then you will attract more stressful situations in your life. In Day 1, you created a desire list for long term goals. Today we are going to focus on manifesting small day to day things like getting coffee without standing in a big line at the coffee shop, getting a parking spot easily, and receiving an adorable gesture from the person we always have a dispute with. Think about any task, thing, or situation into which you are putting effort but not getting the desired result.

The inventions, technology and gadgets we use today were the thoughts and desires of someone who brought them to reality to benefit the world. Everything in creation is a manifestation of one mind. We all are gifted with a super-mind free of limitation and restriction and this mind, working beneath the level of conscious intelligence, is capable of manifesting anything it desires. When we deal with material things, we deal with results, not causes; we know that all causes exist in the mind. The scientific approach to problem solving works from effect to cause. If your mind is focused on the infinite possibilities it will discover a solution to the problem faster[97]; vast opportunities will come to you; a person may show up to guide you to achieve your desire. You have to develop a mindset that is very busy in seeing the possibility of everything going right. It will be filled with gratitude and joyful feelings for yourself and others' success. Gratitude and happy feelings help your mindset to find logic and solutions to cope with day to day life problems. You can achieve a blissful day every day!

Gratitude fills your mind with peace and the more you rely on gratitude the easier life becomes for you. We suffer more in our minds than in reality. All negative thoughts in our mind are obstacles to manifesting our desire. The ultimate form of manifestation is finding a new way of looking at an old problem. Your manifested desire is the result of your mindset. Don't wait for the magical moment to happen; create it with your mindset. When you have gratitude, your mind becomes convinced that you can do something about difficulties and astonishing results will begin to show up in your life. Your mindset possesses all the power you need to solve all the problems in your life.

Today you are going to choose a situation or task in which you want to get the desired result. Your job is to imagine the desired final result or outcome in your mind clearly and express gratitude for it. Think

THE MINDSET

about an area in your life which you want to improve or change. Take a pen and paper and make a list of things that are most important to you or that you want to change. Name this list, "ALL DONE WELL!" When you are done with your list, focus on today, and one at a time imagine clearly in your mind that it is done. Focus on the end result. It is not your job to generate the series of events to take place as you want. All you should focus on is the final desired outcome. Fill your heart with the feeling that it is done, and express gratitude for it being done right. Spend at least one minute on each of your items, believing it is done, and feel massive gratitude in return. Your mind is utilizing its power to bring forth each desire on your "ALL DONE WELL list."

To attract more good things into your life you have to emit a thought and feeling of good outcomes. According to the law of attraction, you attract what your mind emits in the form of vibration in the universe. You have to become a magnet of good feelings to have better life experiences. Being grateful for the solution to your problems helps to attract solutions easily into your life. Remember your mindset becomes a magnet first, and manifestation is a byproduct of a magnetic mindset.

Let me share an example of my friend who experienced the power of ALL DONE WELL List. My friend is a good baker and used to do business from home. With the help of mindset teaching, she started getting more orders. She was overwhelmed with orders which were difficult for her to manage and soon she asked me to let her bake in my kitchen. Her mindset was filled with worry, and she was focused more on negative outcomes like the cake box falling off before it reaches the customer, cup capes not being a perfect size, or the kids not liking the cake decoration. Due to this type of thinking she started messing up her baking and was so frustrated. She was disconnected from gratitude.

When she came to my house, we had a conversation and I asked her to focus on the happy faces of clients and kids. Imagine they are enjoying your baking products. You can have your own bakery. She had more orders to fill so she just relaxed and said thank you for all orders done right. At that moment, the idea struck her to create an online ordering system so she would spend her time baking rather than answering calls. In the next step, she needed a big oven or 5 ovens to bake different products for orders on the same day. It was the time of the pandemic and people were restricted to their houses and taking help from someone was a big deal.

She continued to imagine that all her orders are ready on time and she expressed gratitude for orders done on time. In the next two days, she received a call from a restaurant owner who, thanks to the pandemic, was working alone and needed part-time help to fill his online orders. She agreed to help and asked if she could use a big oven in the restaurant kitchen to bake her orders. He agreed! She delivered all her orders on time and also got a good tip for the work. She focused her mindset on the desired outcome which brought forth the solution for her to make it in time.

Your mind possesses a great power for life which is better than your imagination. You just have to believe in yourself and learn to use it effectively without dwelling on any negative emotion.

THE MINDSET

DAY 21 TASKS

1. Count your blessings: Make a list of ten blessings. Write why you're grateful for each one. Reread your list, and at the end of each blessing say thank you, thank you, thank you, and feel as grateful for that blessing as you can.

2. Create a written list of the things or situation you want to change in different areas of your life. Title your list "ALL DONE WELL!"

3. Choose one item at a time from your list and imagine it is done for you. Clearly see the desired outcome in your mind.

4. Spend at least one minute on each item and focus on each small detail of the desire outcome and how you feel after completing it or receiving it. Express gratitude for it in return.

5. Before going to bed, hold your gratitude rock in your hand and say the words thank you, thank you, thank you from the bottom of your heart for the best things that happened during the day.

DAY 22
CREATE YOUR OWN HAPPINESS

"You can manifest the life you truly want with clear intention, emotional intelligence, and imagination... like it or not, your life is what you have chosen."
– Gregg Branden

The more you practice gratitude, the more your mindset is filled with happiness. Feeling happy is very simple. Material things will not bring happiness to you. What makes you happy is your own thoughts and feelings[98]. To live a happy life, you don't need money, success, or material things. You do need a happy mindset to bring those things into your life. Mindset is the key to true happiness. If someone's presence is making you happy then think again. You are giving away your power to others to control your happiness, and your happiness is your responsibility[99]. You become what you dream of when you embrace who you are. Your mindset makes you whole. Fill it with gratitude and you will thrive.

Be receptive to more than you can imagine for yourself by expressing gratitude for it in advance. Stay devoted to your happiness and you will create your miracle. Scientific studies have shown that happy people are healthier and have a better immune system, live longer, and are better able to overcome adversity. **The only two sources of a happy life are gratitude and good thoughts**. Whenever you face a difficult moment, situation or bad feelings, repeat to yourself.

THE MINDSET

"MY HAPPINESS AND GOOD FUTURE IS MY RESPONSIBILITY."

If you are counting your blessings and doing gratitude rock practice every day then you will wake up happy and energetic every morning. This means gratitude is at work and your mindset is mastering the art of a happy life. Things won't get better unless you thought them better well in advance. Only you can create your happiness. You will experience winning in every situation if your mindset is focused on good feelings, good thoughts for yourself and for everyone. Be your own change. When your mindset is committed to doing the work that creates what you desire, your blessings will manifest. Trust that one day you will be filled with so much happiness that where you are won't matter. Good things won't find you unless your mindset is focused on manifesting it.

"Every day we have plenty of opportunities to get angry, stressed or offended. But what you're doing when you indulge these negative emotions is giving something outside yourself power over your happiness. You can choose not to let little things upset you."
—Joel Osteen

You must be happy now to bring happiness into your life through the law of attraction. It's a simple formula. Happiness attracts happiness. Yet people use so many excuses not to be happy. They use the excuse of debt, the excuse of health, excuse of relationships, and excuses for all sorts of things to show why they can't use this simple formula. But the formula is the law. No matter what the excuse, unless you feel happy despite it, you cannot attract happiness. The law of attraction is saying to you, "Be happy now, and so long as you keep doing that, I will give you unlimited happiness."

Christian D. Larson has written a beautiful happiness poem in his book The Optimist's Creed[100]. Today's first practice is to read this poem at least three times a day and feel happiness, joy for the wonderful life you are going to live in the future. Express your gratitude for the future happiness in advance.

"I promise myself ...

To forget the mistakes of the past and press on to the greater achievements of the future.

To wear a cheerful expression at all times and give a smile to every living creature I meet.

To give so much time to improving myself that I have no time to criticize others.

To be too large for worry, too noble for anger, too strong for fear, and too happy to permit the presence of trouble.

To think well of myself and to proclaim this fact to the world, not in loud words, but in great deeds.

To live in the faith that the whole world is on my side, so long as I am true to the best that is in me."

Write this poem on paper and put it on the visualization board. Make sure to come back to this chapter to read it whenever you feel sad and have bad feelings about yourself.

Today's second practice is to create a journal, notebook, or separate word documents on your computer with the name "HAPPY MOMENTS OF MY LIFE." No matter what day of the month and what month of the year it may be, look back at each month since the beginning of the year and create a monthly happy moments list. Try to write at least three happy moments for each month. Maintain this list till the end of the year and on the last day of the year read all your happy moments. Let's see some examples:

HAPPY MOMENTS OF LIFE

January 2020

1. I traveled to California and had a wonderful vacation which made me happy.
2. I am getting good job opportunities and thriving in my career.
3. I got a new car to travel more. The feeling of traveling in my own car is awesome.

February 2020

1. I have a date. I am happy to celebrate Valentine's day with my love.
2. I started a new job. The feeling of having a steady source of income makes me happier.
3. I have attended so many parties this month.

Maintain it and soon you will see your list of happy moments for each month is increasing.

DAY 22 TASKS

1. Count your blessings: Make a list of ten blessings. Write why you're grateful for each one. Reread your list, and at the end of each blessing say thank you, thank you, thank you, and feel as grateful for that blessing as you can.
2. Write a Happiness poem on a piece of paper or on your computer and read it at least three times today.
3. Put the Happiness poem in a place where you can see it often and make it your habit to read it at least once a day.
4. Create a written list of the happy moments for each month of the year and maintain it. Express your gratitude for those happy moments.
5. Before going to bed, hold your gratitude rock in your hand and say the words thank you, thank you, thank you from the bottom of your heart for the best things that happened during the day.

DAY 23
MIND AND HEART!

"The most beautiful things in the world cannot be seen or even touched, they must be felt with the heart."
—Helen Keller

The main purpose of all gratitude practices you are following now is to feel good about the past and the present and to express gratitude for the future. When your heart is filled with a good feeling it will make you happier and help you to reduce stress. Your mind, heart, and brain work together to give you life experiences[101]. The deeper your heart is filled with gratitude; the greater will be the flow of material things in your life. After practicing gratitude for a long period of time, you will feel it deeply in your heart. Your heart is connected to your mind to generate good feelings and positive stimuli.

To generate thoughts with a well-emotionalized belief, they must be spoken or felt from the bottom of your heart. Your subconscious mind takes the orders generated by feeling in your heart[102]. Hence you must feel good all the time to experience a good life in the material world. **Gratitude you feel deeply helps your heart to have a harmonious rhythm which improves your immune system, overall body health and skin.** We practice gratitude every day to eliminate a negative mindset and behavior from our life so that we can live a happy life.

If you do anything with the good feeling in your heart it will result in success. Our heart is very closely connected to our brain and mind. The heart guides our gut feelings which we should never ignore[103]. It is the system designed to keep our body away from harm. As we learned earlier, bad feelings and bad emotions are harmful to our bodies. You are using a gratitude book and a visualization board to keep yourself focused on your desire. Take a deep breath after going through each desire. This will connect your heart deeply with your desire. The more quickly you master it, the faster your life will become better.

Like attracts like. The more grateful your heart is, the more sincere your feelings. All you have to do is live in harmony with the law of attraction. To do so you have to mold it in your mind, and your heart will feel it with gratitude. Your job is very easy: create in your mind the mold of what you want and feel your heart as though you had already received it.

In today's practice, you are going to focus on how you feel when you go through your desire list. Read each desire on your list one at a time and say thank you three times at the end of each sentence. Close your eyes and focus on how your heart feels. It must feel happy as if you have already received your desire. Express your gratitude for it and feel the goodness in your heart. You can continue this practice on your desire every day to speed up your manifestation. If you practice this every day you will experience increased depth of feeling. The deeper your feeling goes the more the gratitude for it will increase.

"Gratitude is when memory is stored in the heart and not in the mind."
—Lionel Hampton

The more closely your heart and mindset work together the more quickly your life will fill with joy, happiness, and success. Always remember that a grateful heart creates great miracles.

THE MINDSET

DAY 23 TASKS

1. Count your blessings: Make a list of ten blessings. Write why you're grateful for each one. Reread your list and at the end of each blessing say thank you, thank you, thank you, and feel as grateful for that blessing as you can.

2. Focus your mind on your desire and close your eyes and feel deeply the feeling in your heart as if you have already achieved your desire.

3. Go through your desire list one at a time and say thank you three times at the end of reading it. Close your eyes and take a deep breath to fill your heart with joy.

4. Before going to bed, hold your gratitude rock in your hand and say the words thank you, thank you, thank you from the bottom of your heart for the best things that happened during the day.

DAY 24
OUTCOMES

---

*"The most we can hope for is to create the best possible
condition for success, then let go of the outcome.
The ride is a lot more fun that way."*
—Phil Jackson

We've all known those moments when we've said, "I hope this will go well!" These words mean you are expecting a positive outcome, but you are unsure of the outcome. Since you are practicing gratitude, you will understand that your mindset has the power to manifest the desired outcome to anything you want. The universe is all good; however, in difficult situations, we are often not able to see the bigger picture[104]. Even situations we call "Bad" actually have good underneath them. Look at any situation with new eyes and look for the good. If you look for it, you will most assuredly begin to find it, and then you will have burst the illusion of difficulty and allowed all the good to come forth.

If you want a splendid outcome, then you have to fill your heart and mind with the feelings of the outcome as if it is already achieved. Your subconscious mind believes more in emotions and these become your actions to bring the result into the physical world[105]. Your desire first originates in your subconscious mind as emotion and when you achieve the desired outcomes it feeds your subconscious mind with the feeling of pleasure which brings joy and happiness.

THE MINDSET

Sometimes we tend to avoid certain people or situations because we fear the outcome. Fear is a negative emotion which weakens your mind's ability to manifest[106]. To replace the fear, you must fill your heart with gratitude. This will help boost your feelings like courage, inspiration to see an opportunity, good in any situation. You will see life with new meaning and recognize a new possibility which is there for you. Gratitude helps you to reconstruct confidence, hope, and energy. It will fill your heart with joy and happiness. The thoughts with which you have been impregnated radiate to those around you and they, in turn, help you onward and upward; you attract new associates to yourself and this, in turn, changes your environment; so that by this simple exercise of thought, you change not only yourself but the environment, circumstance, and conditions.

Today you are going to choose any situation, person, or circumstance which you fear. Today's practice is to clearly see the picture of the desired outcome in your mind and express gratitude for it with closed eyes, focusing on good feelings in your heart. Then open your eyes and come back to the present moment and relax that it is done already. You are not going to become attached to the outcome; you just need to flash it in your subconscious mind and come back to your present situation with a relaxed mind. When you close your eyes and imagine the outcome with a grateful heart, you are creating a new reality. Your subconscious mind and the law of attraction do not know whether you are imagining something or whether it is real. And so, when you imagine, the law of attraction receives those thoughts and images as though you were actually living them, and it must return those visions to you. When you are in the place where what you are imagining feels real, you will know that it has penetrated your subconscious mind, and the law of attraction must deliver it.

OUTCOMES

> "When you let go of the need for any and all outcomes life becomes a creative magical adventure."
> —Deepak Chopra

Your mind must believe that life is easy, that it is a blessing, and that you deserve all good things life has to offer. You must be open to the outcome and not attached to it. There are many ways an outcome can manifest which you do not see. You just have to think about the end result, not how it is supposed or going to happen. You can be grateful for small outcomes like regular meetings, appointments with the client, parking spots, etc. If you come across any situation unexpectedly, don't feel bad about it; instead, think that it is guiding you towards better things.

Let me share with you my example, I had an important meeting at work for which I had to commute to another office location. There are very limited commute options because it is a suburban area. I missed the train that morning due to some accidents in the area. Instead of beginning to panic about getting there, I closed my eyes and with all my heart said I am grateful for this event to get something better. I was patiently waiting at the station and just across the street, my old school friend was grabbing a coffee. She noticed me from the distance and called me. I was so happy to see her. While talking I got to know she was working in the same office building where I have my meeting. She offered me a free ride and we had a good conversation on the way. As soon as I got into her car, I expressed gratitude for the free and safe ride. I made it in time with a comfortable free ride with my friend. After my meeting, we had lunch together and I had a splendid day.

Most of the time you will see and experience the outcome you asked for and sometimes life will surprise you with splendid result. I didn't know how I was going to benefit from missing the train, but my friend arrived with help to make my meeting successful. When you asked for a magnificent result, and felt sincere gratitude for it, the law of attraction works to bring the result to you, somewhere, at some time. Guaranteed!

Whenever you come across any unexpected situation, or you think you don't have control over something, or you wish for something to turn out well, remember that the law of attraction is working with your good feeling and thinking to bring excellent outcomes. Gratitude protects you from negative situations, bad feelings, and outcomes. It ensures that you get what you want to make you happy.

When your mindset is focused on gratitude, you have the power to change hope and chances into faith and belief. When you keep practicing gratitude it becomes a part of your life, your daily habit, and you will experience only good results in all areas of your life.

Today's practice is to choose any three situations of the day in which you felt you had no control. A visit to a government office where you have to wait, an upcoming interview, a meeting with a new client, meeting new people, a meeting at your kids' school, a community meeting. Make a list of the three situations you have chosen for this activity and use the gratitude in your mind to write an outcome result as if it has already happened:

Thank you for the splendid outcome to visiting the post office!

Thank you for the excellent outcome to meeting my in-laws!

Thank you for the splendid interview result!

Remember you have to express gratitude with all of your heart and once you are done with the practice open your eyes and focus on something else. Don't give it a second thought. Relax your mind as if it is done. Practicing this over and over again will eliminate uncertainty about any situation.

DAY 24 TASKS

1. Count your blessings: Make a list of ten blessings. Write why you're grateful for each one. Reread your list, and at the end of each blessing say thank you, thank you, thank you, and feel as grateful for that blessing as you can.

2. At the beginning of the day choose the three situations or things in which you don't have control and you want to achieve a successful outcome.

3. List your three things, and write a sentence about each one with gratitude in your heart as if it is already happened:

    Thank you for the splendid outcome to..........!

4. Anytime you come across an unexpected event, be grateful for the desired outcome. Each time, close your eyes, observe the good feelings in your heart and say, "Thank you for the splendid outcome to......!

5. Before going to bed, hold your gratitude rock in your hand and say the words thank you, thank you, thank you from the bottom of your heart for the best things that happened during the day.

DAY 25
YOUR MIND WILL MAKE IT REALITY

*"All our dreams can come true
if we have the courage to pursue them."*
—Walt Disney

Four years ago, I decided to leave my country and come to the USA where I have developed a completely different mindset. At that time, I was going through a very bad phase of life emotionally, healthwise, and financially. I decided to take charge of my life and started working on my mindset. I listed my desires and started seeking direction and guidance to achieve them. I expressed my gratitude every time I went through my list. Due to life obstacles I have many times been disconnected from affirmative thoughts but in the summer of 2019 in Boston I finally decided to feed my mindset with only positive and optimistic thoughts which helped me to build tremendous courage in my mind. With continuing practice, I have overcome all fears in my life and life has started to feel like a blessing.

My list of desires was long. Some manifested very quickly and some are yet to manifest. Patience is very important. It takes a long time for some desires, so don't be in a hurry. Hurry will create thoughts of rush and you will end up losing your peace of mind for your desire[107]. Whatever you want will show up if you believe in your desire. You must have a peaceful mindset to move forward. The primary way of achieving a peaceful mind is to empty the mind. The best way to do this practice is to meditate for ten to fifteen minutes during which you don't think about anything. Just go to a quiet place and relax. Close your eyes and concentrate on your heart. Practice this at least twice a day.

You have to build strong gratitude that you have already attained your desire. You have to make gratitude routine in your daily life. Even though I was aware of this technique for a long time, I started my gratitude journal only in early 2020 and still practice it today. As days keep passing, my list of desires started getting short. I tick them each time they manifest and add a new one. Developing your mindset is a continuous process and you have to master it to live a blissful life every day. I made a digital note of my list of desires on my phone and I carry it with me every day. I look at it at least three times a day and give sincere thanks in advance for achieving it. I have seen improvements in my life with a daily gratitude practice.

The more you practice gratitude, the more your mindset gives you self-confidence. Here is the self-confidence formula to improve your mindset towards affirmative life[108]:

1. My mindset has the power to bring all I desire into my life effortlessly.
2. I have understood the principle of autosuggestion that any desire I persistently hold in my mind eventually manifests into reality.
3. I have cleared my mind and focused it on the definite desire list. I will never stop trying until I have developed sufficient self-confidence for its attainment.
4. I will eliminate hatred, envy, jealousy, selflessness, and cynicism by developing a love for all human and natural life because I understood that negative attitudes towards anything will not bring me success.

Remember the above formula and read it today at least three times. Whenever you feel down, come back to this page and read it until you get over the sad feeling.

Now it's time for you to bring all your desires to reality. Live your dream life. Take the top ten on your list of desires and read each of them. At the end of each sentence, visualize in your mind that you have already achieved it. Spend at least one minute on each desire. Carry your desire list in your pocket, purse, wallet, or on your phone everywhere you go. Go through this practice as many times as possible every day. You will soon see each desire pricking your eyes with tears of joy and you will feel happier. Also, after manifesting your desire don't cross it off the list but tick it with the right mark.

Note How to mark your desires:

~~Thank you for the new car.~~ Wrong

✘   Thank you for the new car. Wrong

✓   Thank you for the new car.

DAY 25 TASKS

1. Count your blessings: Make a list of ten blessings. Write why you're grateful for each one. Reread your list, and at the end of each blessing say thank you, thank you, thank you, and feel as grateful for that blessing as you can.

2. At the beginning of the day, read the confidence formula and go through your top ten desires.

3. Read though each sentence and desire on your list, and for one minute imagine or visualize that you have received your desire. Feel as much gratitude as you can.

4. Carry your desires list with you today in your pocket. On at least three different occasions in the day, take out your list, read through it, and feel as much gratitude as you can.

5. Before going to bed, hold your gratitude rock in your hand and say the words thank you, thank you, thank you from the bottom of your heart for the best things that happened during the day.

DAY 26
JOY OF GIVING

*"We make a living by what we get.
We make a life by what we give."*
—Winston S. Churchill

Have you ever felt joy after doing a charitable act or helping someone in need? Many times, in our life we think that we can do something to change the life of others for the better. Today you are going to learn how you can use your mindset to change others' lives for the better. When you wish to help someone, you have the power and when it is blended with gratitude you will see the path or resources to make it happen. If your intentions are good to help others, direct your gratitude power towards another person's need. Gratitude is an invisible energy, but you can experience it and you can use it to help others too.

"The wise man does not lay up his own treasures. The more he gives to others, the more he has for his own."
—Lao Tzu

It is not necessary that you should have to give always in monetary terms. The joy of giving is all about the little help you can pass on to others[109]. You don't need to be wealthy to offer help or send your blessing to someone you care about. You just need a good heart with good intentions to practice gratitude to make a difference in others' lives. Here is something you can do that is one of the most powerful uses of the law of attraction. This exercise is very simple. From today onwards it is your mission to make every single person's day better with kind thoughts and words. Give joy, a smile, warm words, love, appreciation, and compliments to everyone you meet, including strangers, friends, and family. Speak from your heart, giving the very best of you in every moment of your day. As you give the best of you, you will be staggered by the speed that it comes back to you. **Blessing is nothing but a good emotion with good intention ignited in your heart for others**[110]. If you can attract a good fortune to yourself with your mind power, you can also send a good vibration to others for their goodwill. You can attract so as you can reflect on good thoughts.

As a kid in our bedtime stories, we always heard that a fairy will come and bless people and a witch curses people.

The pixie utilizes her power to show you a serious image of your future abundance life, and a witch utilizes the same power to show you awful things. You are not going to be a fairy with wings flying to solve other people's problems magically. Make it a habit to bless everything. Bless and appreciate your home, each member of your family, your work colleagues, your friends, food, nature, animals, and everything that surrounds you. Bless everything in your life, and as you do so you will have ignited the law of attraction into powerful action for all good to come to you. The law will respond by delivering unlimited blessings into your life through people, circumstances, and events that will have you standing in awe.

In today's practice, you are going to choose three people for whom you want to send your blessing through gratitude. Someone in your family, friend circle, or at work needs help in finance, health, relationship, or to gain confidence. Close your eyes and imagine that person is healing from the illness. This person is giving you news about their financial gains. The other person is overcoming the relationship heartache. Imagine the happiest version of that person you want to see and say thank you. It may sound funny, but the power of gratitude and your mindset will bring powerful results soon. If a person you know is going through a tough time, but you don't know what specifically they need, or if they need help in more than one area, then you can use the same practice by giving thanks for their happiness or their happiness in all areas of their life.

Today choose three people who are very important to you or you know need help. Take their photographs if you have them, hold them in your hand and close your eyes. Visualize in your mind that you are receiving the news that the person has been restored with whatever they need. If you visualized yourself celebrating their fortune that will help you to feel more gratitude. Now open your eyes with the photo of that person in your hand and say thank you three times.

And write:

Thank you, thank you, thank you for _____Name___ health, wealth and happiness.

As you finish with one person, move on to the next person, until you complete your JOY OF GIVING practice on all three people you have chosen. Complete this practice at once for all the three people.

The power of giving is greater than the joy of receiving. Using your mind-power with gratitude to bring joy into other's lives or wishing good for others' health, wealth, and happiness will multiply the same things in your life. It's a law! Giving is the highest expression of our mind power. Giving in monetary terms means you have an abundance of wealth and hence you will receive back more abundance. By giving joy, money, or a gift you are setting gratitude power into motion to bring back more of those things to you.

"Giving opens the way for receiving."
—Florence Scovel Shinn

DAY 26 TASKS

1. Count your blessings: Make a list of ten blessings. Write why you're grateful for each one. Reread your list and at the end of each blessing say thank you, thank you, thank you, and feel as grateful for that blessing as you can.
2. Choose three people who you care about and who you would like to help with more health, wealth, happiness, or all three.
3. If you have the photos of all three people, keep them in front of you while doing joy of giving practice.
4. Take one person at a time and hold their photograph in your hand. Close your eyes and for one minute visualize receiving the news that the person's health, wealth, or happiness having been fully restored.
5. Open your eyes and, with the photo in your hand, say thank you three times and utter the words," Thank you, thank you, thank you for ____Name____ health, wealth, or happiness." If possible, write it on the piece of paper.
6. **Repeat steps 4 & 5 for the remaining two people. Do this practice for all the three people at once.**
7. Before going to bed, hold your gratitude rock in your hand and say the words thank you, thank you, thank you from the bottom of your heart for the best things that happened during the day.

DAY 27
SUCCESS IS MY DESTINY

"The universe is a friendly place."
—Albert Einstein

With the practice of gratitude, you have to experience creating your own life with your thoughts. It is a tendency of the human mind to become that which you habitually imagine yourself to be[111]. Success is nothing but a thought ignited in your mind. As soon as you commit to making something happen, the "how" will reveal itself in front of you. As soon as you have thought of success in a particular project or area of your life, be grateful for it as if it is done. When you do this, the universe by the law of attraction start working on it. It will bring signs, situations, people, and events to surround you with the "How" you asked to achieve your victory.

What you want already exists in the universe, but it is waiting for your commitment, thoughts and action to bring success to you[112]. Be grateful life offers a second chance for everything, fresh starts, and unlimited opportunities to change course. You have to claim your success well in advance and be grateful for it before it happens. The universe also chooses its, time to give you what you want because sometimes it takes us time to handle a greater victory. When you feed your mind with positive thoughts it works to have positive surroundings around you to bring positive results. The definition of success is different for everyone but to be grateful for success is common for all.

The universe is constantly working to give us the clues to follow the path for our success. To see these signs, your mind must be at peace and your six senses should be very alert[113]. This will come to you gradually with long-term gratitude practice. Let me share my experience. I was looking for a job in the IT industry and applying for more than one hundred jobs a day on various job portals. One day I was walking through a nice area near the Charles river. I went and sat down there. I wished for a job in nearby buildings so I could have a beautiful view of the city every day. I closed my eyes and imagined the view of Boston from the top floor of the top building and imagined how my office should look like in my mind. I did this for the next few days sitting at the same point. All the buildings in that area are either hotels or malls. A day later, I saw a company name on my LinkedIn profile. There was no job available for my skill set but it was located in the same area I took a walk a day ago. When I met my friends that day two of them told me about the same company. The next day I got a call from a consultancy for a job role. I send him my resume but there was no response. I kept expressing gratitude for a job in the company and clearly saw in my mind the picture of my sitting place and the view from my office window. The universe was working and sending me clues to get a job in the company where the exact view I had imagined was available. I got a job in a small firm near the Charles river and on the first day when my supervisor walked me to my desk, I saw the exact view with my eyes. The universe worked to bring success to me with clues. I closed my eyes and expressed gratitude for it before starting work.

Be aware of your surroundings because the law of attraction is constantly working to make your life better. When you hear an ambulance siren it is a clue to be grateful for good health. Whenever you hear a police van or fire brigades, be grateful for your safe home and neighborhood. When you see someone reading the newspaper it is a sign that good news is going to come soon. When someone wishes you GOOD MORNING, be grateful for the morning because you are still alive.

If you want to buy a car and see your dream car passing by be grateful that you have it. If you are looking for a life partner and see a couple, it is a sign that you will meet your life partner soon. If you pass by an ATM or bank it is a signal to be thankful for the money you have. When you receive a call from a friend or family member, be grateful that you have someone to care for you. The universe is always around you with the right clues to be grateful for at that moment. When you wake up every morning and see the sunshine, it is a clue to be grateful for the life you have. When you go to bed at night it is a clue to be grateful for all the good things that happened that day.

When you are afraid of something, it is a powerful feeling. By the friendly universe law of attraction, it will bring more fearful thoughts and situations to you. Also, it will keep your desire away from you because your mind is focused on fearful thoughts. You have to remove the feeling of fear and use that powerful energy to direct into the possibility of what could go right? Think more about what good things can happen rather than what could go wrong? No matter how you are feeling, every situation, fear, and negative emotion can be replaced in your mind through powerful thoughts. Your good emotions are your power to create something new.

In today's practice, you are going to notice at least seven clues from the universe and say thank you three times every time you notice one. If you are looking for the perfect weight and you see a person with that same weight say thank you for my perfect weight! You have been developing your mindset for the past 27 days; you will have reached a point by now where you will be more alert about your surroundings and notice the clues to achieving success coming your way. The more you practice gratitude, the more your senses are alert and the more easily you will bring your dreams into reality. The universe will provide abundantly when you're in a state of gratefulness.

DAY 27 TASKS

1. Count your blessings: Make a list of ten blessings. Write why you're grateful for each one. Reread your list, and at the end of each blessing say thank you, thank you, thank you, and feel as grateful for that blessing as you can.

2. Today, be alert of your surrounding and take at least seven gratitude clues from the events in your day. Example: if you see your dream car passing by, say "Thank you for the perfect car!"

3. Before going to bed, hold your gratitude rock in your hand and say the words thank you, thank you, thank you from the bottom of your heart for the best things that happened during the day.

DAY 28
MISTAKES ARE BLESSINGS

"There are no mistakes, no coincidences. All events are blessings given to us to learn from."
—Elisabeth Kubler-Ross

Every single mistake in our life helps us to move forward. The past mistakes make you who you are today. Without those mistakes, you would not have gotten so far. In today's practice, we are going to find the hidden blessings in our past mistakes.

As a child, when we fail to learn we practice it again and don't give a second thought to why we made the mistake. As an adult, we make mistakes and we learn from them[114]. Our mistakes make us wiser people. We won't grow unless we heal and, to heal, we need to overcome hurt. Hurt is a negative emotion and your mindset needs to be free from it. We are human and we have a choice of freedom as well as to make mistakes. Mistakes are there to teach us lessons. These lessons are necessary to advance our life. If you don't learn the lesson, the same mistake will keep repeating in your life[115].

You have to accept the fact that you can make a mistake and you have made mistakes in the past. In my life, I made the wrong choice of education because of which I have suffered a lot in my career. I accept I was completely responsible for those mistakes that happened in my life. Due to those mistakes I met many good people in my life and grew as a person. It is very easy to blame someone for your mistake but that will not help you to heal. You should own your mistake and look at it as a good thing. Today you are going to choose a mistake from the past which hurt you and you are going to list what you learned from that mistake and be grateful for it. **Always remember that any bad situation, bad time or mistake is there to guide you towards a better life**[116]. Not all storms come to shake you but some storms clear your path. Back in India, I had a very bad life in terms of relationships with my family, financial crunches, and an unsatisfying career. All these situations forced me to leave the country to start a better life. When I came to the USA life was tough initially, but I took responsibility for everything and never looked back. All those heartaches made me very strong emotionally, and today I am stronger than I ever was before.

Our mind has the ability to turn mistakes into blessings. With the help of gratitude, you can turn any mistake into a blessing. No matter how bad the mistake is. ignoring it and not healing it will weaken your mind's ability to look forward to a better future. There is always something to be grateful for in each mistake[117]. Like attracts like, and mistakes will attract mistakes while blessings will attract blessings into your life. You have to turn all your past mistakes into blessings so that, whenever you look back, you will smile at the blessing you received, and your mind will be at peace.

Today you are going to choose one mistake which still hurts when you look back at your life. It may be the loss of a person, a financial loss, a wrong decision, a wrong career move, or education. Once you have chosen your mistake, look for the things to be grateful for. To help you, there are two questions you should ask yourself:

What did I learn from that mistake?

What good things happened in my life because of that mistake?

The important thing to be grateful for about every mistake is that there is something to learn from it. Each mistake is a blessing. It came into your life to alter the course of action and make your future better. An example of someone who made her mistake a blessing is Oprah Winfrey. She had a very painful childhood and adolescence,

THE MINDSET

but she learned from it and her career as a TV host turned what she learned from those mistakes into a blessing. Every blessing you find from your mistake has power over your mindset. Write in your gratitude journal or make a list of ten blessings.

Let's look at an example of how to turn mistakes into blessings.

If you had a broken marriage, and are now dealing with your life alone.

1. I am grateful for the law because it gives me freedom to live my life rather than being abused.
2. I am grateful that this marriage didn't work out because I came to understand my self-worth.
3. I am grateful to be free from the man who doesn't deserve my love.
4. I am grateful for a new start in my life.
5. I am grateful for the experiences I had in this marriage that will make my next marriage a success.
6. I am grateful for my divorce because I have learned the value of financial freedom.
7. I am grateful for my marriage experiences because I am now clear what qualities I should look for in a partner.
8. I am grateful for my marriage experiences because there are fewer chances of flaws in my next relationship.
9. I am grateful for the divorce because now I have more time for self-development.
10. I am grateful for my children through this marriage because they are a beautiful reason to live for.

Keep practicing this if you regret more mistakes in the past. It is self-healing. You are doing this practice to release the burden from your mindset. The more optimistic your mindset, the more good things it will bring to your life. Seeing mistakes as blessings will help you to look at mistakes differently and learn the lessons to excel in later life. In future, when you make a mistake (and you will, because everyone does), come back to this chapter to find the blessings in that mistake.

DAY 28 TASKS

1. Count your blessings: Make a list of ten blessings. Write why you're grateful for each one. Reread your list, and at the end of each blessing say thank you, thank you, thank you, and feel as grateful for that blessing as you can.
2. Choose one mistake you made in your life.
3. List ten blessings you're grateful for as a result of making that mistake and write them down.
4. To help find your blessings, ask yourself the questions: What did I learn from the mistake? and what good things came out of the mistake?
5. Before going to bed, hold your gratitude rock in your hand and say the words thank you, thank you, thank you from the bottom of your heart for the best things that happened during the day.

DAY 29
ALL ABOUT YOU

"The only person I can change is the person in the mirror."
—Russell Wilson

When we draw a circle, we hold one point, steady to draw a big or small circle. It is that constant point that creates the circle. Similarly, you cannot change the whole world, but you can change your mindset[118]. Once you've mastered your mindset to be optimistic you will see a whole new world around you. The real difficulty is to overcome how you think about yourself and gratitude will help your mindset to overcome it. When you are grateful for being the person you are, you feel good about the self you see in the mirror. The person in the mirror is the worth of all good things, life has to offer.

When you are grateful for the person in the mirror and have good feelings about yourself, that's all you need to change your situation. Negative feelings about yourself cause more damage to yourself than any other thing. A bad mindset about your appearance or your life is more damaging than the bad feelings you have about anything or anyone else. Those tiny feeling of dissatisfaction become a magnet to attract more bad feelings of dissatisfaction and discontent in all parts of your life.

If you have followed the 28 days of mindset practice until this point, your mindset has changed a lot! It is hard to see the changes in yourself; you will have felt a change in your happiness, in situations around you, and in the people around you. You have practiced

THE MINDSET

mindset power for your work, success, health, money, friends, and family. You have learned to deal with unexpected situations in your everyday life. But the person who deserves gratitude more than anyone else is you. If you are filled with love and joy you will pour the same things into the outer world. You cannot pour from an empty cup. If you feel good inside it will reflect in more good things appearing in your life.

When you are grateful for how you are, more good circumstances will show up in your life to make you feel good. Gratitude for yourself enriches you! Life is no longer just happening to you; you are creating it with your mindset. Remember the great secret:

"Whoever has gratitude (for themselves) will be given more, and he or she will have an abundance. Whoever does not have gratitude (for themselves), even what he or she has will be taken from him or her."[119]

Our mind acts on the system of vibration[120]. Our good thoughts create good feelings and give birth to ideas which become our actions and ultimately our life. So, make sure you have a clear picture of HAPPY YOU in your mind. Once it is clear in your mind, it will materialize the outer world for you to be happy.

In today's practice, you are going to use a mirror. Take a piece of paper and write the following sentence in capital bold letters and stick it on the mirror in your house.

"I AM AN AMAZING AND ALLURING PERSON."

From today onwards, whenever you see yourself in the mirror, read the above sentence out loud and say the words thank you three times. If you are not in a position to saying it aloud then just read it and say thank you three times in your mind. You have to name at least three good qualities about yourself. Say thank you for being yourself! Feel grateful for your presence and appearance. Be grateful for you just as you are!

Continue mirror practice throughout the day every time you see yourself in the mirror. If you love yourself, appreciate yourself and then others will do so, too. In future, if you forgot to be kind to yourself, you know to give to the one person who deserves your gratitude more than anyone else – the person in the mirror!

Once your mindset is on the frequency of gratitude you will forgive yourself if you make a mistake. You will appreciate yourself and criticize when you are not perfect. When your mindset is focused on gratitude for being you, you will feel happier and you will attract more happy situations and people into your life. When the mindset of the person in the mirror is changed the whole world around you will change! Your life is all about you and you are the creator of your life.

"BE THE CHANGE YOU WISH TO SEE IN THE WORLD."

THE MINDSET

DAY 29 TASKS

1. Count your blessings: Make a list of ten blessings. Write why you're grateful for each one. Reread your list and at the end of each blessing say thank you, thank you, thank you, and feel as grateful for that blessing as you can.

2. On a piece of paper write in bold capital letters, "**I AM AN AMAZING AND ALLURING PERSON,**" and stick it on the mirror of your home.

3. Every time you look at yourself in the mirror read it aloud and say thank you three times and mean it more than you ever have before.

4. If you look at yourself every time in the mirror say at least three god things about yourself and feel grateful for it as much as possible.

5. Before going to bed, hold your gratitude rock in your hand and say the words thank you, thank you, thank you from the bottom of your heart for the best things that happened during the day.

DAY 30
MINDSET IS EVERYTHING

You have learned how to start each day with a good mindset and go to bed every night with a happy mindset in thirty days. Your mind is gifted with tremendous power to change any situation in your life. You have experienced that satisfaction and gratitude are powerful emotions that are essential to your thriving[121]. They have healing and magnifying powers that can transform your hopefulness into happiness, joy into ecstasy, peace into harmony, and little into plenty. Focus on the good in your life and use appreciation to amplify your ability to attract more abundance and wellbeing. Whatever you want you can make it happen with your mindset. You can count your blessings every morning or go through the flashback of yesterday's good memories. Counting your blessings is the most powerful practice to set your mindset on a blissful, joyful frequency. With your thoughts, gratitude, and mindset you can make every day a successful, happy day.

A positive good thought in your mind is like a new life. When you are constantly on the frequency of good thoughts in your mind it fills your heart with a feeling of joy and your body becomes a magnet for joy and miracles. Constantly imagining yourself into a happy state, a successful you will thrive on the joy and the law of attraction will start working. It will show you the path and tell you how to become happy. You have an experience that your thoughts are an unseen magnet connecting you to the law of attraction. One should remember to keep the mindset focused in the right direction. You should always think more and more happy thoughts for yourself as well as for others[122]. Life is very simple and based on our mindset. Your mind possesses creative thinking power to bring health, riches, or success into your life. You have to think in a certain way which will guide your actions to bring everything you want into your life.

All you need is to focus your mindset on the things you have received, things you have and things you are going to receive with imagination and gratitude. When you practice gratitude every day, the law of attraction comes to your service. Every thought can be made strong and efficient by holding strong vision in your mind as you are doing it and putting your FAITH and PURPOSE into it[123]. Like attract like, so make sure your thoughts are always good for yourself as well as for others. The law of attraction is reflecting and giving back to you exactly what you are focusing on in your mind. With this powerful knowledge, you can completely change every circumstance and event in your entire life, by changing the way you think.

You can let your imagination go wild with a vision board, and place pictures of all the things you want, and pictures of how you want your life to be. Make sure you put the VISION BOARD in a place where you will see it every day. Feel the feelings of having those things now and be grateful for them in advance. As you receive, and feel gratitude for receiving, you can remove pictures and add new ones. This is a wonderful way to introduce children to the law of attraction.

Today's practice is for the moment you wake up in the morning. Go through yesterday in your mind and count the day's blissful events. Note down all the good things that happened to you yesterday. Ask yourself: Did I have a successful, happy day yesterday? As soon as you ask this question, your mind will start looking for the answer and counting your blessings from yesterday. Note down all yesterday's blissful events of on a piece of paper or on your computer. Remember, each day is a new opportunity to start afresh, so do something new for which your future self will be thankful. You have made a journey of one month setting your mindset to focus on a good frequency. You have learned to see the true blessings of life, your heart is open for gratitude, your mindset is set for good thoughts, and your life will be abundant and magnificent.

We all spend our lives acquiring wealth and health which is going to leave us upon our death. Our wealth will go to the next generation and our body will remain in the grave. The only true treasure our soul is going to carry with it is our Mindset!

YOUR MINDSET IS YOUR REAL TREASURE!

DAY 30 TASKS

1. Count your blessings: Make a list of ten blessings. Write why you're grateful for each one. Reread your list, and at the end of each blessing say thank you, thank you, thank you, and feel as grateful for that blessing as you can.

2. On a piece of paper write down yesterday's blessings and make it your habit to repeat this practice along with counting your blessing until you feel satisfied that you had a blissful day.

3. As you note down each of yesterday's blessings, say thank and feel gratitude in your heart.

4. Before going to bed, hold your gratitude rock in your hand and say the words thank you, thank you, thank you from the bottom of your heart for the best things that happened during the day.

DAY 31
COMMANDING YOUR FUTURE

"Gratitude makes sense of our past, brings peace for today, and creates a vision for tomorrow."
—Melody Beattie

With this thirty day's practice, you have learned that you are the creator of your life. With continuous gratitude practice, you can set your mindset in the right direction. You have learned to train your mindset to look for good in every situation. Making gratitude part of your life, you can create anything you wish for. The universe is filled with infinite opportunities if you have the right mindset. **Your future needs you more than your past, and it's your responsibility to always look forward with a grateful mind**[124]. You have created the foundation for your successful life, and it is important to keep working on your list of desires and dreams. Nothing in nature goes backward, so focus on the future. The mental attitude that ensures success is one in which the individual turns his thinking and action over to the universe without attachment or desire.

All you have to do is focus your mindset on what you want and be grateful for it in advance. You have worked to build a new mindset in this thirty day's practice. You have experienced the difference in your happy feelings and the good life around you. The more you practice gratitude, the more deeply your feelings will root to successful, happy feelings about your future. Remember the mindset forever; you have to make it your daily habit to make your life better.

THE MINDSET

Some of your desires will manifest in a few days while some will take a year or more. Do not give up but continue your gratitude. It feels so nice to play the game in your mind about the things you want to materialize. Keep your visualization board filled with your dreams and replace them frequently with new dreams. Teach your kids about gratitude from an early age so that they will have an optimistic view of life and easily manifest success in their life.

Your mindset power increases when you look forward with hope, expecting and demanding better things to come. That is the law of infinite mind, which you follow if you live with a good mindset[125]. Gratitude is fuel to have a focused and optimistic mindset. The science of happiness lies in controlling our thoughts and getting thoughts of the successful life we want to live. If you lack in any area of your life, practice the mindset power more in that particular area of your life. When you practice gratitude, faith and confidence get rooted in your subconscious mind easily. There is plenty for everyone and you must have faith in yourself.

Remember to think good things about yourself and others. If you succeed and earn wealth, you must create an opportunity or path for others to achieve the same. Charity, donations, sharing your knowledge all create a feeling of an abundance and the universe will bring more to you. The more you lift others, the better your surroundings become and one day the world will be full of good people. Whatever you do you must continue practicing to master it.

Remember the autosuggestions you have learned in this book. They are very powerful words to ignite your subconscious mind with affirmative thoughts.

"Every day, in every way I am getting better and better." This sentence is very powerful and you can apply it for anything you want in your life.

"Every day, in every way I am getting better and better in my job or business."

"Every day, in every way I am getting better and better with my health."

"Every day, in every way I am getting better and better in my relationship."

"Every day, in every way I am getting better and better in my skills."

"Every day, in every way I am getting richer and richer."

After every sentence closed your eyes and say the words THANK YOU! three times to feel more gratitude as if you have already achieved it.

"SUCCESS DOESN'T COME FROM WHAT YOU DO OCCASIONALLY. IT IS THE RESULT OF CONSISTENT EFFORT."

If you want to increase a particular area of your life you have to practice gratitude for the past, present, and future. For example, if you are looking to increase your wealth you have to practice a mindset for the money you had in the past, the money you have currently, and the money you are going to receive in the future. Below are a few suggestions on how you can practice mindset focused on a particular area of your life[126].

HEALTH

Past health - Day 19: HEALTH IS A GIFT!

Current health – Day 26: JOY OF GIVING

Future health – Day 31: COMMANDING YOUR FUTURE

CAREER

Past career – Day 9: YOUR WORK

Current Career – Day 20 MONEY MAGNET MINDSET

Future career – Day 26: JOY OF GIVING

THE MINDSET

All about you – Day 29: ALL ABOUT YOU Commanding your future – Day 31: COMMANDING YOUR FUTURE

DESIRE

Past desire – Day 1: DREAMS

Current desire - Day 2: DIRECTION

Day 3: DECISION

Day 16: MIRACLES HAPPENS OVERNIGHT

Future Desire – Day 26: JOY OF GIVING

All about you – Day 29: ALL ABOUT YOU

Commanding your future – Day 31: COMMANDING YOUR FUTURE

WEALTH

Past wealth – Day 8: THE MONEY

Current Wealth – Day 12: FOUNDATION OF ABUNDANCE MINDSET

Future wealth – Day 20: MONEY MAGNET MINDSET

Day 26: JOY OF GIVING

All about you – Day 29: ALL ABOUT YOU

Commanding your future – Day 31: COMMANDING YOUR FUTURE

Whatever the area you are focusing on, repeat the given specific day's practice for four weeks.

HOW TO BREAK THE WORRY HABIT

*"Worrying is using your imagination
to create something you don't want"*
– Esther Hicks

What is worry? It is nothing but an unhealthy and destructive thought in our minds. When you are practicing gratitude, your mindset will stay away from it. I myself got disconnected from my mindset many times and fell back to the worrying habit. It is not easy to break the worrying habit but with practice it is possible to overcome it completely. To get rid of worrying habits you have to calm your mind. We are born with a worry-free mindset, but we acquire it with our thoughts and experiences[127]. As you change your mindset you can get rid of worry completely. You have to fix in your mind that we will never run out of good things because there's more than enough to go around for everyone. Life is meant to be abundant.

The simple first step towards breaking the worrying habit is to believe you can do anything with your mindset. You have to believe that worry is temporary and brings you closer to success[128]. It is there to give you a lesson to bring the best out of you. There is nothing to fear or develop anxiety about worrying. You can empty your mind before you go to bed with gratitude rock practice and you reunite with your happiness by counting your blessings in the morning. Make sure you go to bed with happy, joyful experiences and happy thoughts. In your sleep, your thoughts sink deep into your subconscious mind. The last five minutes before going to bed are of extraordinary importance, for in that brief period the mind is most receptive to suggestion. It tends to absorb the last ideas that were entered into waking consciousness. **Do not scroll thought news or your mobile phone before going to bed. Instead, practice ten minutes of meditation.**

Whenever you are faced with worry or anxiety, try to use your creative imagination in your mindset. Try to project as many good outcome images as possible and express your gratitude for them. You can try this method at any time of the day by going to a quiet place twice every day and doing it for five minutes each time. Faithfully performing this process will bring the result you want sooner. Imagination is a source of fear but also a cure for fear. Day by day, as you fill your mind with faith and gratitude you will reach a point where there is no room for fear in your mindset. You will be blind to defects. Master faith and you will automatically master fear[129]. As you learned to master small worries initially, soon you will easily overcome big worries.

After practicing for thirty-one days, you have experienced the power of the mind. Make sure you keep it up with good thoughts and gratitude. Be patient with your progress. Some of your dreams will manifest easily and some will take time. Maintaining a happy mindset forever will help you to overcome worrying habits. When you have an emotion like fear, your mindset and imagination unintentionally provide the vison for what you don't want. Fear and success are equally powerful. You have trained your mind to look at the good side of everything no matter what you have been thinking or feeling, and your power to create something new is NOW.

You can check whether you are on the right track or simply overserving your emotions. Are you feeling stressed, worried, angry? Does your body ache? Do you wake up in an unhappy mood? Feel tense? If yes, then you are on the wrong track and those feelings are keeping you away from your desire, your dream. You have to be relaxed, calm and not concerned about when, where, and how your desire will be manifested. Every time you think about your dreams and desires you must have happy feelings in your heart, mind and body. You need to relax, relax and relax deliberately till you feel happy about it. To master this will take time.

Gratitude is my way of life now and I cannot imagine life without it. If you disconnect from the gratitude practice your mindset power weakens and you fall back to the downside of life. I have repeated this downfall cycle many times in my own life but finally, in the year 2020, I made it my life and my life changed forever. I feel grateful for every situation, and obstacles just disappear from my way. My mindset is to see good in every situation.

To get complete control over your mind you have to calm it first. There are various techniques to calm your mind, but the best and easiest way is not to think about anything and to focus on your breathing. Inhaling and exhaling for ten minutes will help you to calm your mind.

THE MINDSET HERO

After 31 days of practice, you will sense a difference in your feelings. You have become a happiness magnet. This technique works for everyone because the laws of the universe treat everyone equally.

If you are interested in being featured on our website, you can submit your story (1000 words max) to http://mindsetbymayura.com/tell-us-your-story and we will post it in our Mindset Heroes section. You can include your photo if you wish.

We look forward to learning about your experience with The Mindset metamorphosis!

ABOUT THE AUTHOR

Mayura Shekatkar grew up in India surrounded by adverse situations and negativity. In 2015, she started reading about optimism and her 2016 arrival in the United States was the major turning point in her life. Research coupled with personal experience revealed to her the way to a happy and blissful life. Her writing is inspired by her own experience of developing an optimistic mindset towards living. She wrote her first book, "The Mindset" during the 2020 pandemic. Mayura holds the degrees of Master of Science in Information Technology Management and MBA in Human Resources. Apart from writing, she works as an HRIS Analyst for a firm in Boston, MA. In her free time, she volunteers at an animal shelter.

Follow her on:

YouTube: https://youtube.com/channel/UCbGYWDTddSAyvZ5n_5dvhBA

Instagram: https://instagram.com/themindset_mayurashekatkar/

Pinterest: https://pinterest.com/themindset0154

Facebook: https://facebook.com/themind.mayurashekatkar/

Website: http://mindsetbymayura.com

ENDNOTES

1. Byrne, Rhonda. *The Magic*. Atria Books, 2012. 1.
2. Mulford, Prentice. *Thoughts are Things*. CreateSpace, 2016. 33.
3. Byrne, Rhonda. *The Secret*. Simon & Schuster, 1994. 177.
4. Byrne, Rhonda. *The Magic*. 3
5. Peale, Norman Vincent. *The Power of Positive Thinking*. Touchstone Books, 2003. 11.
6. Hill, Napoleon. *Think and Grow Rich*. Sound Wisdom, 2016. 210.
7. Peale, Norman Vincent. *The Power of Positive Thinking*. 212
8. Hill, Napoleon. *Think and Grow Rich*. 234-235.
9. The Dalai Lama & Cutler, Howard C. *The Art of Happiness: A Handbook for Living*. Riverhead Books, 2020. 139.
10. Hill, Napoleon. *Think and Grow Rich*. 231-232.
11. Haanel, Charles F., *A Book About You*. Kallisti Publishing, 2008. 119.
12. The Dalai Lama & Cutler, Howard C. *The Art of Happiness: A Handbook for Living*. 139.
13. Hill, Napoleon. *Think and Grow Rich*. 118.
14. Larson, Christian, *Your Forces and How to Use Them*. CreateSpace, 2008. 65.
15. Ibid. 66.
16. Ibid. 67.
17. Ibid. 70
18. Hill, Napoleon. *Think and Grow Rich*. 88
19. Ibid. 132.
20. Larson, Christian, *Your Forces and How to Use Them*. 57.
21. Hill, Napoleon. *Think and Grow Rich*. 135.
22. Garcia, Hector & Mirallas, Francesca. *Ikigai: The Japanese Secret to a Long and Happy Life*. Penguin Life, 2017. 42.

23   Mulford, Prentice. *Thoughts are Things*. 44.
24   Ibid. 106.
25   Hill, Napoleon. *Think and Grow Rich*. 159.
26   Ibid. 160.
27   Ibid. 161.
28   Larson, Christian, Your Forces and How to Use Them. 18.
29   Ibid. *Think and Grow Rich*. 187.
30   Ibid. 181-182.
31   Ibid.187.
32   Byrne, Rhonda. *The Magic*. 29.
33   Ibid. 31.
34   Ibid. 32.
35   Ibid. 33.
36   Ibid. 38.
37   Oppland, Mike. "13 Most Popular Gratitude Exercises & Activities." *Positive Psychology*, 9 Jan 2020. https://positivepsychology.com/gratitude-exercises/.
38   Byrne, Rhonda. *The Magic*. 39.
39   Ibid. 44.
40   Ibid. 44.
41   Ibid. 46.
42   Peale, Norman Vincent. *The Power of Positive Thinking*. 42.
43   Garcia, Hector & Mirallas, Francesca. Ikigai: The Japanese Secret to a Long and Happy Life. 37.
44   Ibid. 38.
45   Byrne, Rhonda. *The Magic*. 53.
46   Ibid. 54.
47   Ibid. 57.
48   Ibid. 61.
49   Hill, Napoleon. *Think and Grow Rich*. 177.
50   Wattles, Wallace D. *The Science of Getting Rich*. Sound Wisdom, 2019. 31
51   Ibid. 33.
52   Ibid. 29.

53   Byrne, Rhonda. *The Magic*. 64.
54   Wattles, Wallace D. *The Science of Getting Rich*. 32.
55   Byrne, Rhonda. *The Magic*. 69.
56   Hill, Napoleon. *Think and Grow Rich*. 125.
57   Wattles, Wallace D. *The Science of Getting Rich*. 22.
58   Peale, Norman Vincent. *The Power of Positive Thinking*. 73.
59   Garcia, Hector & Mirallas, Francesca. Ikigai: The Japanese Secret to a Long and Happy Life. 49.
60   Hill, Napoleon. *Think and Grow Rich*. 179.
61   Wattles, Wallace D. *The Science of Getting Rich*. 35.
62   Byrne, Rhonda. *The Magic*. 81.
63   Ibid. 87.
64   Garcia, Hector & Mirallas, Francesca. Ikigai: The Japanese Secret to a Long and Happy Life. 208.
65   Byrne, Rhonda. *The Magic*. 92.
66   Ibid. 5.
67   Wattles, Wallace D. *The Science of Getting Rich*. 32.
68   Honda, Ken, "Arigato Money Technique from *Happy Money*." 5 Nov 2019, YouTube. https://youtu.be/J3yN8noND-k.
69   Hill, Napoleon. *Think and Grow Rich*. 98-102.
70   Andersen, U.S. *The Magic in Your Mind*. Martino Fine Books, 2017. 81.
71   Ibid. 82.
72   Ibid. 86.
73   Byrne, Rhonda. *The Magic*. 112.
74   Garcia, Hector & Mirallas, Francesca. Ikigai: The Japanese Secret to a Long and Happy Life. 64.
75   Byrne, Rhonda. *The Magic*. 117.
76   Hill, Napoleon. *Think and Grow Rich*. 195.
77   Mulford, Prentice. *Thoughts are Things*. 10.
78   Byrne, Rhonda. *The Magic*. 123.
79   Hill, Napoleon. *Think and Grow Rich*. 41.
80   Ibid. 54.

81 "Number Symbolism: Phythagoreanism." *Encyclopedia Britannica.* 2020. https://www.britannica.com/topic/number-symbolism/Pythagoreanism#ref248160.
82 Byrne, Rhonda. *The Magic.* 134.
83 Haanel, Charles F., *A Book About You.* 27-29.
84 Andersen, U.S. *The Magic in Your Mind.* 86.
85 Byrne, Rhonda. *The Magic.* 138.
86 Peale, Norman Vincent. *The Power of Positive Thinking.* 257.
87 Mulford, Prentice. *Thoughts are Things.* 35.
88 Garcia, Hector & Mirallas, Francesca. Ikigai: The Japanese Secret to a Long and Happy Life. 35.
89 Ibid. 41.
90 Mulford, Prentice. *Thoughts are Things.* 33-35.
91 Peale, Norman Vincent. *The Power of Positive Thinking.* 41.
92 Wattles, Wallace D. *The Science of Getting Rich.* 15.
93 Haanel, Charles F., *A Book About You.* 120.
94 Andersen, U.S. *The Magic in Your Mind.* 71.
95 Ibid. 86.
96 Peale, Norman Vincent. *The Power of Positive Thinking.* 140.
97 Hill, Napoleon. *Think and Grow Rich.* 22.
98 Mulford, Prentice. *Thoughts are Things.* 108.
99 The Dalai Lama & Cutler, Howard C. *The Art of Happiness: A Handbook for Living.* 109.
100 Larson, Christian D., *The Optimist Creed and Other Inspirational Classics: Discover the Life-Changing Power of Gratitude and Optimism.* TarcherPerigree, 2012. https://www.craftdeology.com/inspiring-poem-promise-yourself-by-christian-d-larson/.
101 Garcia, Hector & Mirallas, Francesca. Ikigai: The Japanese Secret to a Long and Happy Life. 20.
102 Hill, Napoleon. *Think and Grow Rich.* 73.
103 The Dalai Lama & Cutler, Howard C. *The Art of Happiness: A Handbook for Living.* 520.
104 Haanel, Charles F., *A Book About You.* 129.
105 Ibid. 130.

[106] Peale, Norman Vincent. *The Power of Positive Thinking.* 111.
[107] Ibid. 26-27.
[108] Hill, Napoleon. *Think and Grow Rich.* 52-53.
[109] Andersen, U.S. *The Magic in Your Mind.* 72.
[110] Peale, Norman Vincent. *The Power of Positive Thinking.* 56.
[111] Haanel, Charles F., *A Book About You.* 157.
[112] Peale, Norman Vincent. *The Power of Positive Thinking.* 212.
[113] Hill, Napoleon. *Think and Grow Rich.* 116.
[114] Peale, Norman Vincent. *The Power of Positive Thinking.* 210.
[115] Andersen, U.S. *The Magic in Your Mind.* 139.
[116] Ibid. 142.
[117] The Dalai Lama & Cutler, Howard C. *The Art of Happiness: A Handbook for Living.* 341.
[118] Haanel, Charles F., *A Book About You.* 120.
[119] Byrne, Rhonda. *The Magic.* 232.
[120] Mulford, Prentice. *Thoughts are Things.* 27.
[121] Byrne, Rhonda. *The Magic.* 213.
[122] Mulford, Prentice. *Thoughts are Things.* 36.
[123] Wattles, Wallace D. *The Science of Getting Rich.* 57.
[124] Mulford, Prentice. *Thoughts are Things.* 44.
[125] Ibid. 45.
[126] Byrne, Rhonda. *The Magic.* 243.
[127] Andersen, U.S. *The Magic in Your Mind.* 163.
[128] The Dalai Lama & Cutler, Howard C. *The Art of Happiness: A Handbook for Living.* 612.
[129] Peale, Norman Vincent. *The Power of Positive Thinking.* 149.

www.ingramcontent.com/pod-product-compliance
Lightning Source LLC
Chambersburg PA
CBHW072016110526
44592CB00012B/1324